Hieros Gamos

Sacred Union of the Divine Feminine and Divine Masculine

Channeled from Mother Mary Anna by Penny Genter

Hieros Gamos – Sacred Union of the Divine Feminine and Divine Masculine
By Mother Mary Anna and Penny Genter

Published in 2016 by JOEF Publishing, an imprint of Journey of Enlightenment Foundation, P. O. Box 21603, Sedona, AZ 86341.

Copyright © by Penny Genter, 2016.

All rights reserved.

Cover image Divine Union available through Creative Commons Attribution Share Alike

ISBN-13: 978—1539517153
ISBN-10: 1539517152

"To love another person is to touch the face of God"

Victor Hugo

Acknowledgements

I wish to thank all of those in my life who have lovingly shown me the face of God, especially in my intimate relationships where there is the greatest opportunity for growth. I especially want to thank "Tom" and "Jerry" for allowing me to tell our intimate story so that others might learn and be inspired to begin their own journey in Hieros Gamos.

I wish to thank my family who have been the perfect mirrors of life and love, ever expressing.

I wish to thank all of my spiritual teachers and guides, both incarnate and divine who have loving shown me the way. I wish to thank especially Michael Mirdad for his guidance on this sometimes-rocky path which kept me focused on the light.

I especially wish to thank all my soul sisters and brothers who have held my hand through this journey – you know who you are…Namaste

Contents

Forward 10

Hieros Gamos 12

Message from Mother Mary Anna 13

Penny's thoughts: 16

The Journey of the Soul Through Incarnations 18

Reincarnation 19

Soul Groups/Soul Mates 20

Dr. Michael Newton 21

Edgar Cayce 21

Paramahansa Yogananda 22

Karma 23

Penny's Thoughts: 26

Communicating with your God Energy 32

Attracting Your Energetic Partner 36

Chemistry 39

Letting Go of Relationships That No Longer Serve You 41

The Ceremony of Honoring and Releasing 42

My Honoring and Releasing Ceremony 45

Creating Healthy Relationships 48

Penny's thoughts: 51

Integrity 52

The Practice of Integrity 53

The Impact of Personal Example 55

The Myth of Romance 56

Preparing for Intimate Relationships 57

Building Trust 58

Ways to Cultivate Trust in a Relationship by Dr. John Gottman 62

Truth 66

Laying the Groundwork for Sacred Partnerships 67

Penny's thoughts: 70

Be Love 71

Penny's thoughts: 74

Understanding our Complimentary Nature 76

Preparing for a Loving Partnership 78

Penny's thoughts: 81

Walking a Common Path 84

Penny's thoughts: 86

Ah Ha Moments 87

Penny's Thoughts: 89

Deepening Experiences of Love 91

Attracting Your Energetic Partner 94

The Gift of our Soulmates 97

Preparing for Divine Partnership 99

The Commitment 101

Divine Intimacy 104

Becoming One	107
Invitation to the Dance	109
The Dance of Beloveds	111
Divine Partnership	114
Conflict Resolution	116
Divine Healing	119
Divine Comedy	121
The Three-Legged Stool	124
Juicing the Ride	127
Divine Communication	130
Sacred Partnership	133
Divine Creation	135
Archetypes of Wholeness	137
Penny's Thoughts	139
Relationships in the New Paradigm	140
Journey of the Chakras	142
At the Door of the Temple	146
Experiencing Hieros Gamos	147
Jerry	148
The Third Possibility	155
The Intimate Dance	157
Health	160
Hieros Gamos	161
Healing	162

Soul Contracts 162

Communication 166

Balancing the Masculine and Feminine 168

Time out 169

Sacraments of Love 170

The Kiss 170

The Embrace 171

Ten More Minutes 172

Ecstatic Union 175

"Hard Drugs" 177

Positions 177

Soaking Meditation 178

Seeing God in our Beloved 180

Commitment 186

Healing Wounds 187

Flower and Gem Essences 187

Depression 189

Control vs. Concern and Caring 192

Honeymoon 194

Decisions 197

Jerry Retrograde! 198

Jerry Direct 200

Lighting the Way for Others 202

Pass it On 206

Finally 208

New Ceremonies of Commitment 210

Mother Mary Anna on Sacred Union Ceremonies 211

In the New Relationship Paradigm 215

A Ceremony of Sacred Union 217

Postscript: 223

Wisdom Keepers in the New Paradigm 225

Note: Titles in italics are channelings from Mother Mary Anna

Forward

My conscious walk with Mother Mary began in 1996. I used to go into bookstores and browsed shelves waiting for something to "fall out in my hands". One day a book, *Opening to Channel* by Sanaya Roman did. I thought "Well that sounds like fun". Little did I know what a profound effect it would have on my life.

I went home, read it and sat down with my tape recorder and prepared to receive. I opened my mouth, and nothing came out. I remembered that Ruth Montgomery had done this on her typewriter so I sat down at my computer. Being a touch-typist, I closed my eyes, asked to be connected. Mother Mary came through, word by word, phrase by phrase. It was very loving and far more eloquent than anything I could write. All I did was spell check and check for punctuation and I now had a hard copy to share with others. We wrote two books together over the next ten years; *Touching Home* which she used to bring me up to speed in spiritual understanding and *Returning Home* with Merlin and Quan Yin which is a workbook for ascension. Then others stepped in to take me in different directions.

In 2006 I became aware that I had shared a previous life with her at the time of Jesus' incarnation. I was Mary Jacobe Cleophas, niece of Mary Anna and cousin of Jesus. I was four years older than her and we grew up together as sisters and life-long friends. I was one of the three Marys at the crucifixion [i]and went with the holy family to France after we were driven out of Egypt.

In 2008 I was led on a Spirit guided pilgrimage to France and found myself guided in the footsteps of Mary Magdalene. We began in Saintes Marias-de-la-Mer. The first thing I noticed upon entering the church of Mary Magdalene there was an effigy of a small boat carrying Mary Jacobe and Mary Salome. Our bones are relics in the church. The adventure continued…

Hieros Gamos

I first became familiar with the words *Hieros Gamos* in the books of Kathleen McGowan and her descriptions of the sacred marriage of the divine feminine and the divine masculine in *The Book of Love*. She describes the *"sacred marriage of trust and consciousness that unites the beloveds into One."*

I found the description of the love affair of Solomon and Sheba profoundly moving and compelling[ii]. This struck a chord deep in my memory and left a bookmark for me to revisit at a future date.

In facilitating the 2014 Magdalene Celebration in Sedona I came to know Mercedes Kirkel. I have been a fan of her work in *Mary Magdalene Beckons: Join the River of Love* and am on her weekly newsletter e-mail list. Her latest book, *Sublime Union* is a personal channeling and account of her experiences in sacred sexuality with her partner. While I found the book authentic and helpful to many people, I kept sensing that this was about healing and energizing the lower chakras but was not the whole picture. I got the integration of the lower chakras but felt there was more involved to integrate the upper chakras with the heart. The morning after I completed reading the book I awoke with the sense that Mother Mary had more to share on the subject. She did…

Message from Mother Mary Anna

My channeling prayer:

I AM Christ Consciousness. I AM Unconditional Love. I AM the Light. Lord Michael and the Rescue Angels come in now and remove all entities not of the Light and take them where they need to go for their soul growth. I direct that I be connected with Mother Mary and that all other entities be excluded from this message. Do you wish to communicate with me about the Hieros Gamos?

(Note – all channeled messages are in italics.)

My dearest sister Penny,

Many years have passed since we strode the dusty paths of Galilee together. It is time for the things that we knew to be true to be shared with the world. It pleasures me to know that despite the passage of time and experience, we still are able to connect so readily at the level of the heart. Your wisdom now, as ever, transcends experience and connects with a higher source.

The teachings passed down through the priestess trainings in the Great Pyramid are being brought forth but there is a critical element that is missing – the connection with the heart and the upper chakras. In order to have a full integration of mind, body, and spirit, it is necessary to integrate not only the masculine and feminine, but to realize the full expression of these qualities in our divine blueprint. This requires healing of the wounds in the lower chakras that can be accomplished with conscious sexual union and appropriate energy practices, but it also requires an engagement of the Loving energy of the heart through the full expression of unconditional Love as we have shown you. It is through this door that access to the higher chakras is integrated into form

We will share with you in the coming months the steps for you to integrate this not only into your own life, but you will have the opportunity to demonstrate this in form with a beloved that will be a lesson for not only yourself but for you to share with others, much as Mercedes has done. It will be about what it looks like to fully activated and integrate the process of Hieros Gamos into form.

While this has been a vague process to many, you will be able to bring this alive for many who are ready to enter this next level of the ascension frequency. You experienced many aspects of this with Gordon, but we will be bringing you to an even higher level of awareness so that you can share it with those with ears to hear. It will be about compassion and honoring; about appreciation and caring on a level seldom known in your world. It will be about coming together in a full aspect of the One with reflection of the divine qualities of the masculine and feminine amplified in a higher appreciation of the divine in each other.

We ask that you remain open to the process, connect with us daily and we will guide you through a journey of loving awareness, process and magnification of the magnificence of divine partnership when fully expressed with the complement of your soul's longing. This is the journey of the soul into reunification with the God spirit that you embarked on in incarnation. It is not a walk in solo but in tandem with your energetic complement so that you can fully integrate these aspects either within yourself or in partnership with another individuated being. The destiny for all is the same and is through the heart of love in its most magnificent form which is the embodiment of the Hieros Gamos. We will share the process and ask you to share your earthly experiences so that others will be able to follow in your footsteps.

Many blessings, my sister. We will have a joyous walk together again, Mary Anna

Penny's thoughts:

How delicious would be the experience of love, lived in its highest expression of divine love and ecstatic pleasure in the arms of the beloved. Just her descriptions of the sacred union of the divine masculine and divine feminine as exemplified by Solomon and Sheba sent shivers up and down my spine and longings in my heart and elsewhere spurred by remembrance from this and other lifetimes of uncompleted experiences of love, longing to be fulfilled. Certainly, there have been other lovers, romances, and marriages which gave me a taste of possibilities, but none that measured up to the level of fulfillment promised in this ultimate expression of ecstatic Love.

When Mother Mary Anna came to me again and asked me to bring through another book with her on *Hieros Gamos – the Sacred Union of the Divine Masculine and Divine Feminine* I was more than interested, especially when she promised that I would have a beloved come into my life that I would be able to experience this with and share my experience with others. As I began receiving her teachings of how we can create this sacred union in our lives, I was struck not only by the beauty, simplicity and profundity of her messages, but how relatively shallow had been most of my experiences in love to date. I wanted to experience the full expression of romantic/erotic/sacred love in my life and would gladly shout it from the rooftops if necessary if I could experience such ecstasy.

Beginning in August of 2014 I received thirty-six messages from Mother Mary Anna on the various aspects of sacred love. I thought I was to just put them together in book form along with my musings, but she had other ideas. She said that there are many kinds of "books". I was led to put together a series of classes using PowerPoint presentations to guide others through the process. It included not only her teachings but sayings and videos and teachings of many of the most important teachers, therapists, ministers, bloggers and just plain folks with their insights on how this is showing up in the new paradigm we are creating.

I presented these to the Unity of Sedona Board of Directors, and they realized the importance of what was being given us and agreed to co-sponsor weekly "Creating Sacred Relationships" classes. It is said that we teach what we need to learn. Still missing the beloved I had been promised, I nevertheless began sharing what I knew and was being shown in the weekly classes, believing that by becoming the love we wish to experience, we attract that energy to us. Those who continued to show up further enriched the process with their feedback and shared experiences. Following are some of the highlights excerpts from the class and from experts in the field:

The Journey of the Soul Through Incarnations

My understanding of soul mates is others in our soul group who have agreed to travel together through lifetimes and assist in each other's growth and understanding. You do not have just one soul mate, though there may be ones you share a deeper commitment to growth together.

I have been asked to share my story, not because I am special or have extraordinary experiences, but because I have the advantage of age and many life experiences which gives me a longer perspective. I am able to see how the parts fit together and reveal a more complete picture of how things work and show up in the dance of life. I am given insights of some of my past-life experiences and can share examples of how these things have manifested in my life, which is always better than talking about things abstractly. I am told this is coded to trigger remembrance of things in your own life path and I encourage you to jot down things that arise for you to go back and examine later. It may also bring up concepts you are unsure of such as channeling, reincarnation, and dowsing so note any questions you may have.

Reincarnation

Reincarnation is the recycling of the soul through numerous incarnations so that the perfection of the god-spirit may be attained. Each succeeding lifetime builds upon the prior ones to experience lesson that can help grow the soul in awareness and increase the energetic vibration until it is perfected into the One.

Reincarnation was part of the teachings in ancient times and certainly at the time of Jesus. It wasn't until the Roman church decided that it threatened their authority that it was dropped from the teachings.

"The soul returns to earth in a body similar to its last one and has similar talents and inclinations." – Plato

Soul Groups/Soul Mates

Our soul group/mates come to earth with us and some of them work behind the scenes on other dimensions. They come as mothers, fathers, teachers, friends, the plumber, etc. that are here to grow, learn, and ascend together. Any soul that you connect with deeply could be considered a soul mate. People can have many soul mates. Usually, they are individuals who have similar rays and spiritual paths, and often have been together for many lifetimes off and on. Since many of us decide to incarnate together for the purpose of growth and transformation, when you find others that you have been with before, there is a high probability that this is not the first experience together. Frequently it is through the eyes of others that we are able to discern the colors and textures of life that go unrecognized alone. By blending and merging with others that have agreed to share experiences on the earth plane, we are able to recognize and embrace more than if this were a solitary journey. It is a group process and a higher form of teaching and learning.

Dr. Michael Newton

Dr. Michael Newton talks about the contracts we make between lives with each other to meet up and be mirrors for each other's soul growth. We give signals so that we will recognize each other.

Edgar Cayce

We know from the study of Edgar Cayce's readings and other sources that successive future incarnations should have at least five key points of similarity

1. Astrology
2. Facial Appearance
3. Karmic traits and lessons
4. Karmic places
5. Karmic people

Though it may not be easy to trace a connection through astrology, quite often we feel we know another through their facial appearance even though we have not met them in this incarnation. We usually find professions and interests that relate to our previous experiences. We are drawn to places and people with whom we have shared previous lifetimes.

Paramahansa Yogananda

Paramahansa Yogananda said that there is a way that you also can recognize those whom you have known before. "We may associate with some people day after day, yet never really know them or feel close to them. But there are others with whom we feel immediately a deep harmony the first time we meet. It is not anything physical. It is a memory of the past.

Many, many people that I have met in this country, and in India and elsewhere, I have known before. The friendship is even stronger now. It was not finished in past lives, and so it had to continue to evolve in this life. Friendship is the highest form of love. As such, it is meant to evolve into the divine manifestation of God's eternal love. Friendship is the highest relationship, because in friendship there is no compulsion; it is born of the free choice of the heart. It is God calling souls back to unity in Him. If you can be a friend to all, unconditionally, that is divine love. Not many in this world find true friends; mere acquaintances are not to be confused with real friends. There is no attachment in true friendship, nor is it founded in selfish human love. It is an unconditional relationship between two or more souls: they may be unrelated, or family members, or marriage partners. It is best formed between souls who are seeking God or who have found God. Such was the friendship that existed between Christ and his disciples. Otherwise, relationships develop into attachment and remain on the plane of human love, taking the soul away from supreme friendship with God."

Karma

"When speaking of relationships with others, there are generally only two kinds of relationships – karmic relationships (cell mates) and gifting relationships (soul mates)". (Michael Mirdad, *Creating Fulfilling Relationships*)

Most karmic relationships are not easy. Two people are brought together to learn how to unselfishly love one another, heal past life imbalances and wounds and express their authentic self. These relationships are usually initially passionate and stir up deep feelings of longing and what feels like love. This irresistible magnetism is usually needed as these relationships can be challenging. Past emotional wounds, fears, anxieties and egocentric selfishness often surface. There may be periods of harmony and loving connectedness interrupted by conflicts, power struggles and unfounded fears. Simply put they can be confusing. Despite the desire to leave a karmic relationship, the magnetic attraction may keep pulling you back. The soul chooses these difficult relationships because of their inherent potential for healing, growth, wholeness and to refine and experience real love.

Karma can be painful – but as you learn more about your life, through both your wonderful and painful experiences, you will grow wiser and more whole, and the pain will ease. Just being aware of the karmic nature of the partnership will lessen its power over you. Once you assert yourself or take charge of the situation in a conscious way, you'll feel the burden slowly lift. Communicating your needs and wishes, not tolerating unkindness, sticking up for your opinions and beliefs, and most importantly, forgiving yourself, will melt those binding karmic ties into oblivion. Once you have learned your lesson you will know in your heart that you will never have to deal with that particular piece of karma again.

When you meet someone, you have a karmic connection with, a spark of recognition ignites in your soul. You'll feel a haunting familiarity, a sense of having come home, a longing for something not quite remembered. You might recognize their face, name or the sound of their voice, or you may intuitively know you have met before. If this person is a potential lover, these feelings are magnified, giving the whole relationship a compulsive, alluring intensity. You'll feel a connection that goes way beyond what you actually say and do together. Something profound appears to be bubbling away under the surface.

If you have karma to resolve in a close relationship you may be sucked into a whirlpool of repetitive patterns and behavior that appears to have very little to do with your conscious wishes and actions. But because you know the pattern, you're compelled to repeat it. Karma has to be compelling and addictive, otherwise you wouldn't learn anything from it. Its only purpose is to teach, so you can become more whole.

In a karmic relationship between two conscious people, the existing karma may be harmonious. Two people come together from a previous life where they have worked out their ego centered challenges and love one another with a pure and compassionate love. In these relationships both people often come back together to work toward a common goal. Usually this goal is to be of service to others and contribute to the greater good. Their authentic self has been integrated into the relationship and they can freely and joyfully be with one another.

Penny's Thoughts:

Much of what happens in this incarnation has its roots in previous incarnations. When we learn to see things from this broader perspective, many of our relationships begin to make sense. I know that my prior life that ended at age six in Dachau led to my strong beliefs about injustice, shunning and religious tolerance. But it was the incarnation prior to that in the Impressionist period in the latter part of the 19th century in France that has provided much impetus for my study of reincarnation and soul groups.

In 2006 I was awakened in the night and guided to a book on Renoir on my bookshelf. Turning to the picture of *The Luncheon of the Boating Party*, I was told who I was (the man in the straw-hat leering at the woman in the upper right corner) as well as others in the painting. Over the next few years I got pieces in downloads of a whole soul group that had traveled through time together, reincarnating at significant times in history. This was cool because Renoir was such a prolific painter and portrait artist. He painted all his friends and fellow painters, politicians, movers and shakers of the period. It is so well documented I was able to put together faces and names of who they were then and those I know now in New Mexico and Arizona.

I came to learn that in that time, I was a man, Paul L'hote, close friend and travel companion of Renoir, the Impressionist painter. I was a lifelong bachelor, bon vivant, adventurer, and lover of many women. I certainly brought into this lifetime much karma from that one. I can trace many of my relationships with men is this timeframe to encounters we had then and many of the lessons I have learned from them. Karma can be a bitch sometimes, but it does work if we use these insights as opportunities to learn and grow. You may want to trace your akashic roots for lifetimes that significantly impact this one.

My father died when I was five setting the stage for dealing with abandonment issues that continued throughout my life as I buried three husbands. Given that I had spent a recent incarnation loving and leaving women, it began to make more sense. As I became more self-aware, that was no longer an issue.

I came from a family of women who provided wonderful role models but there were no models of the masculine in our lives. My main views of that world came on TV with shows like *Father Knows Best, The Donna Reed Show,* and *Leave it to Beaver*. With no one to show me anything other than this idealized view of the masculine, I believed all men were good, noble, and loving. I was curious and wanted that in my life. I married young and quickly had four babies.

Karma had greater lessons for me. My husband was manager of a store in Houston, TX. The estranged husband of one of the women who worked for him came in, he got in the way and was shot and killed. Even at that young age, I knew that I was not willing become a victim and let that define my life. My children and I deserved something better. I did not understand it then, but now I know; my husband had been one of the women I loved and left in that previous life.

I was working as a secretary at IBM where I was able to study in-house to become a computer programmer. I eventually got a job as a computer systems analyst at NASA Manned Spacecraft Center in Houston where we helped put a man on the moon. This is where I met my second husband. He had one son and was more aligned with my images from TV as to what a good husband and father should be like. We lived out another soul contract together as we raised a family moving around the country to Washington, DC, northern and southern California and finally New Mexico.

He became depressed and refused to get help. We finally divorced after 26 years of marriage and he sat on the couch until he died a few years later. Abandoned again but this time I was stronger and more confident. He was also part of the soul group represented in the *Luncheon of the Boating Party*.

Then I met Gordon, another face in the painting. We had each been married 26 years; each had five children, three boys and two girls each. Fortunately, they were all grown. At first he wasn't even sure he was supposed to be with me because he "had been in metaphysics for 25 years and I was such a newbie" even though I had been in love with God my whole life. He came to regret that early assessment big time and became my greatest supporter, advocate, and promoter as we learned together the real meaning of unconditional love.

I became a quick study, or I believe, a quick "rememberer", as many of the teachings from previous lifetimes were reawakened in my awareness. This is when Mother Mary came back into my life, and we began a magical journey together. I also became an ardent and proficient dowser which opened the door to communication with the other side even wider.

We went to Findhorn and Paris on our honeymoon. I designed and we built a geodesic adobe together in the mountains of New Mexico, with a mandala garden, labyrinth and three ponds. We created a flower essence business together and had a conscious communication with Nature. He produced the books Mother Mary was giving me. We learned, grew, loved and honored each other in so many ways and found ways to share this with others with ears to hear.

Then seven years into the marriage he got pancreatic cancer. It was horrible but at the same time beautiful. We don't often have the opportunity to share with those we love the full depth and breadth of that commitment. This was the gift in that I was able to be there for him and to reflect all of the lessons in unconditional love that this was affording us.

We cured the cancer holistically using all of the alternative tools in our arsenal. They did three CT scans and could not find the tumor. But I believe that when the soul decides it is time, you can maneuver the body, but it will find a way to exit. He eventually developed blood clots in both legs which is what finally allowed him to exit this lifetime.

He was conscious until almost the end and we were able to celebrate our life and our love together. Our children and grandchildren came from all over the country. We had a life celebration ceremony with a shaman where he was the honoree. We laughed, cried, ate together and laughingly shared the incredible journey it had been. We had a *bon voyage* party with friends and neighbors with kids on the bed sharing joys and beliefs. We were able to openly share the love we had in our hearts for each other and appreciate how he had helped us to realize that. When he finally stopped breathing, we were complete.

Love never dies though it may change form. Three days after his transition, I began channeling his spirit. I continued to channel him for the next five months as we continued to reorient into our new lives. Then he said that I had moved through the grief, he had work to do with the White Brotherhood, and for me it was time to begin "kissing frogs". I said I wasn't sure where frogs were these days and he said, "on the internet". And that is where my journey continued and eventually led me to Sedona.

Though I had kissed a few frogs, I had not yet met the beloved that Mary Anna told me was coming. I only knew that if I became the beloved I would like in my life; I would attract that to me.

Communicating with your God Energy

I remember the first time I discovered that I could ask questions of my God/Higher self and actually receive answers back. It changed forever my experience in the world and gave me the focus and direction to chart a path without the distraction of indecision. The key to this, as with everything, is getting out of the ego and opening to divine wisdom and inspiration. When we get out of our own way, let go and let God chart the way, miracles can occur.

The second most important skill, in order to tap into this inner wisdom, is learning to ask clear, concise, yes-or-no questions. Convoluted, muddy questions get unclear results. It is a process of mental clarity, focus, and breaking down complex situations into mini components that will be affirmed as either positive or negative. By placing yourself outside this realm of possibilities, you can see more clearly the patterns taking form and the reasons behind the choices.

Third is belief that you indeed are connected to this inner (God) wisdom. Perhaps you need to "fake it until you make it" which may be connecting and testing for answers for all things in your life and acting on these insights until you believe in their validity. What should I wear today? Should I have the chicken or fish for dinner? Is my son telling the truth? Should we go to the mountains or abroad on vacation? All of the things in our life come into sharper focus when we operate in the truth of our being. You don't have to know why, just believe that it is in your highest and best good and move forward.

I believe it is important to connect with the right station if you want to listen to the right program. I prayerfully ask to be connected to God, Mother Mary Anna, the Deva of Flower Essences or whatever energy I wish to tap into the wisdom of and that all other entities be excluded. It is my way of dialling into the right channel and not have a lot of interference on the party line. I also state my alignment (I AM Christ Consciousness, I AM Unconditional Love, etc.) so that information come through with that intention.

Once you have the "ear of God", there is nothing that is beyond your reach. Your mental, emotional, spiritual, and physical health are open books to be examined and healed. The secrets of this, and all other lifetimes, are hidden in a locked box but you now have the key. Like the story of Pandora's Box, do not open anything unless you are prepared to deal with the outpouring. When you are ready, there is a gift with your name on it.

This does not mean that you will live a charmed life on clouds of joy and wonderment. It does mean, however, that you will have the tools and road map, if you choose to use them, to navigate a higher path of awareness, avoid many pitfalls on the journey of life, and complete many lessons you came here to master.

All of existence is based upon a complex energy matrix, connecting all life. Things that enhance our well-being have a positive vibration; things that are detrimental have a negative energy signature. By calibrating or dowsing the energy of something, we know whether it is life-affirming for us or not. This may be an experience, supplement, healing modality, person, or anything that interacts energetically with us.

There are many techniques for doing this. You, your health care practitioner, or chiropractor may use tools like muscle testing of indicator muscles that respond with either strength or weakness when subjected to the energy of something – food, medication, supplement, or diagnosis. You may prefer using dowsing tools such as L-rods or a pendulum. All are valuable when used properly, which means getting out of your own way without placing a thumb on the scale through your doubts or beliefs. If you are working with others, you will want to voice your queries aloud, but these work on an internal level as well. As with any skill – practice, practice, practice.

One that I have found most beneficial to master, because you can use it anywhere and do not need tools, is O-Ring testing. Machaelle Small Wright describes this in her book, *Flower Essences, Reordering Our Understanding and Approach to Illness and Health.* As she says, "It allows us to discern what we need and don't need, despite what we think. And about getting that kind of accurate feedback, we learn more about ourselves." You set your intention to use your body to reflect the energy of anything (substance, whether you are physically in contact with it or not, relationship, idea, etc.) This is easy to use in the grocery store to see which produce is best.

In his book *Power vs. Force*, Dr. David Hawkins showed us how to calibrate truth on an energetic scale. You can test for positive or negative responses for the subject numerically on a scale (1-1000). Things that calibrate over 500 are good for you, less than 500 not. I frequently use this to confirm and evaluate things I feel, read, or hear that may be beyond the perception of the other five senses.

Many find it easier to get out of their own way using a pendulum. I like the pendulum also because it gives a third possibility - unable to process with the given information. For me this means it goes in a circle rather than back and forth or sideways. If it refuses to move, it means the answer is blocked for some reason. With any type of energetic testing, it is important to get a baseline, so you know what positive and negative responses look/feel like for you. You can ask "show me a yes" and "show me a no" or say something you know to be true, such as your name, and something you know to be false. Practice until you are comfortable with the process.

One of the challenges in using this new paradigm tool for decision making in a relationship is that both parties need to be comfortable with the process. If not, it may require lots of communication as each partner explains how they came to their realization about something until both are on the same page. Ideally it should be an appreciation of the tools each brings to the process which can unite the perceptions from different sides of the brain.

Attracting Your Energetic Partner

If you feel that you are in this world but not of it, this is essentially so. Around you are those who are struggling in opposition to each other because they have not opened the door to the heart which is the passage to peace and tranquility. We might suggest that your journey will be calmer if you choose to surround yourselves with those who reflect the same level of peace, tranquility, and Loving acceptance as you do. If you wish to share an energetic frequency, learn to distance yourselves from those who do not share that vibratory level.

As to how this plays into choosing a romantic partner, we might suggest that while you may be attracted to others who are members of your soul group, there will be one who possesses the energetic wiring to connect in sacred partnership. This will not prevent your learning about discernment from the others, but the one who matches you energetically will be, without question, the best match for you in not only vibration (attraction), but have the missing pieces that will enhance and empower you on your higher path. Those with whom you will have to compromise your goals, values, and desires in order to come together in relationship are not the best match.

As for purpose together, this does not necessarily mean that both must have the same vision. In fact, both may have complementary parts to each other's. Far more important is that the vibrational frequency and level of spiritual mastery should be compatible in order to assure that they will be working together rather than in competition or distance.

Physical attraction is a process of attunement. One feels in the other missing frequencies in their own energetic wiring. While this is beyond the cognitive reckoning of the third-dimensional mentality, it is a significant factor and something that is known in your world as "chemistry". It is the magnetic frequency that draws one to another and begins the dance of Love.

Awareness of the attraction is only the beginning. In lower forms of awareness, this may be confused with LOVE, while in fact it is only the invitation to go deeper. Once you have each other's attention, it behooves you to begin exploring the other at a soul level. What are the qualities present or missing in the other that compliments your own? How might you weave them together in the dance of love? What are the motivations and constraints that define the other? Are these compatible with your own? Are the joys you experience in being together worth the struggles that will be required to heal the longings and woundings of the heart?

While this may sound cold and distant, when compared to the distractions of unbridled desire, it is in fact part of the deeper process of loving awareness. It is looking beneath the paint and glitter of emotional lust and ascertaining if this is the soulmate for which we have been searching. It requires sharpening our own perceptions as to who we are and what we not only desire but need at a soul level in order to complete our dance card of experience. It is strengthening our ability to look into the soul of another and ascertain what is required and how we might achieve it. It is removing the rose-colored glasses of infatuation and seeing clearly if this person is capable and willing to travel together and take the higher path of sacred partnership.

Most are not for they have not reached that level of spiritual maturity, but when you have raised your vibration to that frequency, you will magnetize to you those who have a compatible energy. Allow your preconceived notions of what the ideal relationship should look like and you will attract to you the beloved your soul has called into the dance. Begin to see each other as radiating beings of light and that will be your experience and your reality. This is the promise of your soul...

Mary Anna

Chemistry

There are different levels of chemistry. Sometimes it is slow and drawn out and becomes more powerful over time but more often it is an instant feeling that blindsides your existence. Chemistry is something that you feel uncontrollably and is just one step further in the passion department but is more powerful than lust. When you can feel someone's energy matching yours and the sexual endorphins are released, nothing is as powerful! Sometime the pheromones are so powerful that it actually pulls you towards them like a magnetic force. There is a magic in the air, and it is an unmistakable euphoric feeling.

What are the signs?
- There is an overwhelming urge to be close and touch them. It is like an electric current that is pulling you into them. It is not always at the right moment, it can be with someone who is out of bounds, but it is an undeniable feeling hard to ignore!
- Nervousness that you are not used to feeling
- An arousal in the loin area
- An amazing urge to kiss them right there on the spot.
- That you are willing to sleep with them as quickly as possible despite your strong morals
- Their scent is overly alluring & draws you closer
- You are drawn into their eyes & have trouble focusing on what they are saying

Due to the magnitude of the electrical current some people tend to step over their boundaries. Acting first and dealing with the repercussions later.

Wikipedia says: "Lust is the initial passionate sexual desire that promotes mating and involves the increased release of chemicals such as testosterone and estrogen. These effects rarely last more than a few weeks or months."

Evan Mark Katz says: "I'd like you to consider that the effects of lust and attraction have been hurting your chances of finding love. What you'll notice is that when you're incredibly attracted to someone, all of your critical thinking powers immediately go out the window. This is why you'll put up with a man who only calls you once a week, a man who doesn't call you his girlfriend after three months, a man who doesn't propose after three years. If you were thinking critically, you'd never put up with this, but you're not. You're under the biological effects of lust and attraction – hereby known as "chemistry". And all I'm pointing out is that while chemistry is an incredible feeling, it is in no way a solid predictor of your future. It's literally just a feeling. A feeling that masks your partner's worst traits and allows you to put up with them."

"Relationships have only one main purpose with two parts: 1. Sharing love 2. Learning about and removing all obstacles to that love." (Michael Mirdad, *Creating Fulfilling Relationships*)

Letting Go of Relationships That No Longer Serve You

"Expressing unconditional love does not mean that no matter what the circumstances, we have to continue a particular relationship. Having unconditional love means that if we part ways we will remain committed to refusing to blame or judge the other person. Also, we will continue to affirm the spark of light within that person." As we develop a healthier, more authentic sense of who we are, we are more likely to meet others who mirror this healthiness and authenticity back to us, thus increasing the odds of having more success in our relationships"

"Probably the only thing worse than staying in an unhealthy situation longer than necessary is not being aware that it is an unhealthy situation." (Michael Mirdad, *Creating Fulfilling Relationships*)

No relationship is ever a waste of time. If it did not bring you what you want, it let you know what you don't want.

The Ceremony of Honoring and Releasing

My dearest sister Penny,

You have come far in embracing what we suggested to you and are now ready to put some of the procedures into practice. For those that have not used ceremony before, I would like to make a few suggestions:

First before doing a ceremony or ritual, it is important to clearly define the purpose. If it is to complete a phase of growth and release each other in love, that should be clearly stated. It is best to have all of the parties present and fully engaged but if they are no longer incarnate or at a physical distance, inviting them in and acting in their surrogacy is appropriate also.

In any ceremony of a mystical nature, it is helpful to join all forces of the omniverse to work together in carrying out the intention. As you prepare an altar, you might wish to include representations of the earth energies and elements including fire, water, earth, air, sound, minerals, metals, plants and animals.

Think of the purpose in what energies you wish to create. What symbols might represent prosperity, disillusion, travel, separation, graduation or other passages or intentions in life.

Create a place of interaction such as an altar or tabletop where the focus can be fixed for all in attendance to gather around.

You may wish to begin by calling in your higher selves, angels, teachers, guides and spirits from the seen and unseen realms to be part of and support in the mystery. You may wish to sound a gong, cymbal or bell to signal beginning of the ceremony.

Leave all questioning thoughts behind, intend, and believe that whatever is transpiring is in divine order. This is a process of trust that allows you access into the higher dimensions where love is the key that unlocks the door. This is a space where past hurts, judgments and projections are dissolved and categorized as lessons that got you to where you are today. This is a place of BEing in a loving environment of peace.

Once all of the fears and anxieties of the ego are dissolved and all are in a space of loving energy it is time to do the process of the dismantling of the past. You may wish to have cords that are wrapped around a central candle that represents the journey together, with separate candles at each end that represent the participants. There may be more cords if there are more than two who are part of the ceremony as appropriate.

Each of the participants should light their own candle then together use those to ignite the central candle. As appropriate, each participant will take turns expressing the blessings and understandings they received by being part of the central association. All take turns expressing the things they learned from the experience and how they were able to shift into greater understanding of their own lives, thanks to the participation, conscious or not, of the other party(ies).

Again, in alternate turns, each should take this opportunity to express gratitude for the, sometimes painful, lessons they provided each other that helped them reach higher on the spiritual path.

When all are finished it is time to unwind or sever, whichever is appropriate, the cords that link one to another. As this is done, each might wish to repeat, "I release you in love from this commitment and experience." Together they should blow out the central candle.

After bowing in Namaste, you can blow out your individual candles. You may wish to shake a rattle, ring a bell, sound a gong or light incense to disburse this energy to the ethers.

While this concludes the ceremony, it may be appropriate and meaningful for each to share their individual experiences with each other in loving ways.

In your world there are few such ceremonies of release resulting in resentment, anger and misunderstanding being carried and nourished, eating away at the soul and physical body of the participants. Many diseases of the body have their origins in the energetic seeds planted in the emotional body. The universal antidote for all pain and dis-ease is love, fully and completely expressed.

We hope this gives you and others ideas as to how you might use ceremony to release any impediments to experiencing the full flowering of Hieros Gamos in their lives.

Your loving sister, Mary Anna

My Honoring and Releasing Ceremony

Tim and I dated for about six months. There were many things that drew us together, not the least of which was our proficiency as communicators, and willingness to hear and learn from each other. He moved to Sedona to explore our relationship together. Towards the end, though we still had a great love and respect for each other, we knew that we were not energetically compatible. He returned to California.

Tim and I had continued to keep in touch. I had shared with him my feelings about why I thought things had fallen apart in our relationship and he pretty much agreed but offered few insights from his end. He was reluctant to say anything that would cause me distress but in doing so he created a void that was open to misinterpretation. We had agreed to love each other unconditionally which meant that we also wanted the best for each other, regardless of how that might affect us personally. If this meant friendship and not lovers, then so be it.

However, there had been no completion or closure to the process, and everything had been left unsaid and therefore ambiguous. We all read between the lines, highly influenced by our hopes and dreams. I had been reluctant to change my status on Facebook because I was not sure exactly how things stood between us. On my way back from California I stopped in for a visit.

There is no question that this continues as a loving relationship with great appreciation for each other but the parameters and definition of what that looks like have changed. Given the perspective of time and distance we were able to share what was going on for us and why we believed we acted as we did – and what we learned about ourselves from it. We were able to thank each other for the part we played in creating this and how it had allowed us to grow in loving awareness. He shared how this was helping him in his search for a new partner and how a woman he has found is helping him heal other aspects of himself and he was doing the same for her.

I asked him if he would be willing to go through the honoring and releasing ceremony with me and he agreed. As a psychologist he recognizes the value of attaining closure and the power of such a ceremony.

I laid out an altar on the coffee table. I chose candles of equal height because we are equals in the relationship. I represented elements of the world we live in and influence – air, fire, water, earth, metal, sound, flora, and fauna. I laid out intentions in the prosperity frog, Chinese figure of good luck and long life, rose quartz crystals for Love and the crystal pyramid symbolizing our path through the chakras to the divine. In the center I placed a candle representing our relationship. Around it wrapped cords symbolizing our attachment and interweaving energies with each other on this path.

We began with the sound of the bowl, calling in our higher selves and guides, and stating the intention of the ceremony of honoring and releasing each other in love. We took turns thanking each other for the gifts we had received in the relationship, what we had learned and our hopes and good wishes for the other. When we felt complete we unwound the cords saying, "I release you in love". We blew out the center candle together and then our individual candles. A heartfelt Namaste, shaking of the rattles and chiming of the bowl completed the ceremony.

Following the ceremony, after the hugs we spent some time staring into each other's soul and processing the meaning and importance of what had taken place. I finally was ready to change my Facebook status.

Creating Healthy Relationships

As you move into a relationship based upon loving awareness, you will notice a shift in the frequency of your interactions. While you may still notice the other's "faults" they will morph into something more akin to facets of their being that will be etched away as you come into closer alignment with their divine aspects. We come together in intimate relationships partially so that we can smooth off these rough edges and help refine and polish the soul qualities of the other. When you see your partner as an aspect of the divine and hold them in the image of that perfection, all that does not match will gradually drop away because it no longer conforms and serves no purpose.

Many of the defense mechanisms we adopt are merely to test the other to see if they are genuinely loving to us and able to overlook these barriers we have put up to prevent our being hurt again. As the need for protection becomes obsolete, the defense mechanisms that were there to shield the fragile heart are no longer necessary.

In many ways, giving of the body may be easier then opening of the heart to another. When you remove the inner clothing of the heart, you bare your soul to the scrutiny of the other. What have you been reluctant to reveal about your inner process, motivation, or dreams that masks the real longing of your soul? Perhaps this is the purpose of your journey together, to allow the uncovering of the misconceptions that prevent the full flowering of your soul gifts.

There are many reasons for our intimate relationships but most of them are about healing wounds that we have carried with us from previous incarnations and families of origin. The opportunities for healing and understanding are heightened when we open our hearts to the tender embrace of the beloved where they are able to apply the salve of loving kindness and facilitate true healing of the wound.

The first priority for lovers in search of this heightened experience of mystical union should be the examination of the woundings that they came together to heal. Realization of the impediments to surrender to the other is the first step; expressing to and acceptance of each other's challenges to intimacy is the next. Integration requires a commitment of both to be the healing agent of love in each other's journey to wholeness.

Growth occurs when we become the healing balm of nurturance and agency by which each of the partners are committed to walking together on a healing path. Sacred partnership requires a common commitment to this process rather than seeing it as "your problem". Disillusion occurs when the other's challenges are no longer seen as separate, but as mirrors for us that are there to be healed together. If this common path cannot be found, it might be better to part sooner, rather than later, because without that assurance and commitment, the paths are destined to separate until the chasm will be obvious to all.

You might wish to think of yourselves as conjoined twins. An infection in one will ultimately affect the health of the other. You might wish to see this as an affliction of the whole body that will lead to dis-ease unless it is addressed in a systemic way. For health of the emotional bodies which are merging as well, working together to help each other see the hidden parts of an issue will help heal aspects that are hard to see and appreciate alone.

The gift of a soulful, sacred relationship is that this becomes a priority and a commitment so that the ecstasy of Hieros Gamos can be fully realized. Until sacred partners are whole and healed of these primary wounds, it will be difficult to access the inner provinces where Oneness can occur. The commitment of both parties to physical, emotional, and mental health and wholeness assures that both come to the altar of love, ready and able to partake of the feast of celebration of the sacred union of Hieros Gamos.

Mary Anna

Penny's thoughts:

Before Gordon and I were married he was in counseling. This brought up childhood issues that required healing. At that time, I believed that these were his issues that were causing him to behave in ways that impacted me. It wasn't until I became involved in the process and helped him work through what had become our issues, did we begin to move together as loving partners in the relationship. His issues were my issues because they prevented him from becoming the caring, healthy, whole partner I wanted in my life. While I could not "fix" or do the work for him, the fact that I was supportive of his journey into wholeness helped him move into that space. I also realized that this was mirroring to me what I needed to heal so that we could come together as healthy, whole individuals capable of creating a sacred partnership together which we did.

Integrity

"If there is one thing that most often makes or breaks our relationships (in every form) it is our ability (or inability) to take responsibility." (Michael Mirdad, *Creating Fulfilling Relationships*)

"Integrity comes from one who has the courage to act from the wisdom of the heart." (Harrold Becker, The Love Foundation)

"The most important ingredient to a fulfilling relationship is the ability to know how to share love with one another while remaining responsible for our own issues – rather than projecting them on each other." (Michael Mirdad, *Creating Fulfilling Relationships*)

The Practice of Integrity

To live with integrity is to actually integrate what you think, know, believe with what you say; and to integrate what you say with what you do. Integrity also presumes a basic level of honesty, a willingness to look at yourself, to question what you think you know, and to continually look for evidence that what you believe to be true is actually true. This can often take courage. Living with integrity is not something that you have, it is something that you do.

Your integrity is always a work in progress. Living with integrity in the real world would always be impossible without the possibility of doing something morally wrong, learning from it, taking action to correct it, and through integrating the experience, and adjusting your behavior accordingly as you grow and become a better person. When you feel ashamed or disappointed, your decision to live with integrity draws you to look at what you are doing that has drawn you off track.

A commitment to living with integrity involves adopting a few general principles that can serve as guideposts to moral decision-making.

- You decide to value what is true.

- You strive to understand yourself and the world.

- You try to understand others, which requires empathy.

- You know what you value.

- You know what you believe.

- You decide to pay attention to feedback—pain, satisfaction, joy, disappointment, and genuine admiration—that suggest that you have something to learn and integrate.

- You decide to pay attention to these on an ongoing basis.

- If you practice integrating your thoughts, feelings, and knowledge with your words and actions, actively living with integrity, you will get good at becoming more profoundly who you are, and you will have the power of moral clarity and a more unified purpose within yourself.

The Impact of Personal Example

It is not simply wishful thinking that a man with integrity can have a significant impact on the integrity of others. We do not live in a vacuum, isolated from others. The impact that we have upon each other is significant, and in this, the role of a person living with a high degree of integrity is substantial. In practice, what this means is that people are watching. What you do in your daily life can have a very positive—or negative—effect on the people around you. Far from suggesting that you are at the mercy of social forces, this makes a strong case for asserting your own leadership and personal virtue.

When you return that extra change from a miscalculated bill, when you don't go along with others in your group who are willing to fudge data, or appease a bully, or gossip, or intentionally hurt somebody, other people are influenced, and that is very likely to make a real impact.

It is in our day-to-day lives that most of us make our greatest impact. When you decide to disregard the negative status quo; when you live actively and congruently with who you are and what you value, you have a much greater influence than those who allow themselves to be drawn away from their moral center. When you choose to behave with honor and integrity—particularly when other people aren't doing so—somebody will notice and will then be very likely to make a different *and better* decision as a result.

The Myth of Romance

"We focus obsessively on romance, the single most irrational, volatile, and illusionary form of love. We fail to consider that love might be an art involving skills that need to be developed throughout a lifetime. Romance is compounded of equal parts of attention, erotic longing, sexual desire and ersatz adoration created by an idealized imagination. It feeds on images, projections and illusions and it flourishes on the absence of real knowledge about the other. It can exist without any realistic commitment. Romance focuses on what is beautiful, interesting, and desirable and usually doesn't involve a great deal of compassion, repentance, or sacrifice. Romantics and shoppers in the mall in quest of the perfect partner or wardrobe are prey to disappointment because no sooner do they possess the object of their affection than their desire returns and goes hunting for another object to excite it." (Sam Keen, *To Love and Be Loved*).

Just ask the six wives of Henry the VIII.

As men may be drawn to pornography, women may be drawn to romance novels. They both represent unrealistic fantasies/longings unexpressed in their lives. The Romance or honeymoon stage of a relationship is about living in the fantasy. You share hopes, dreams, and possibilities in a relationship. It is the rose-colored glasses of infatuation that is the invitation to the dance. Eventually you begin to wake up to the realities of what that really means in form which is where the dance together begins. When we go immediately to the tango without establishing trust that things get hairy and our lessons come at us full force and we trip ourselves and others.

Preparing for Intimate Relationships

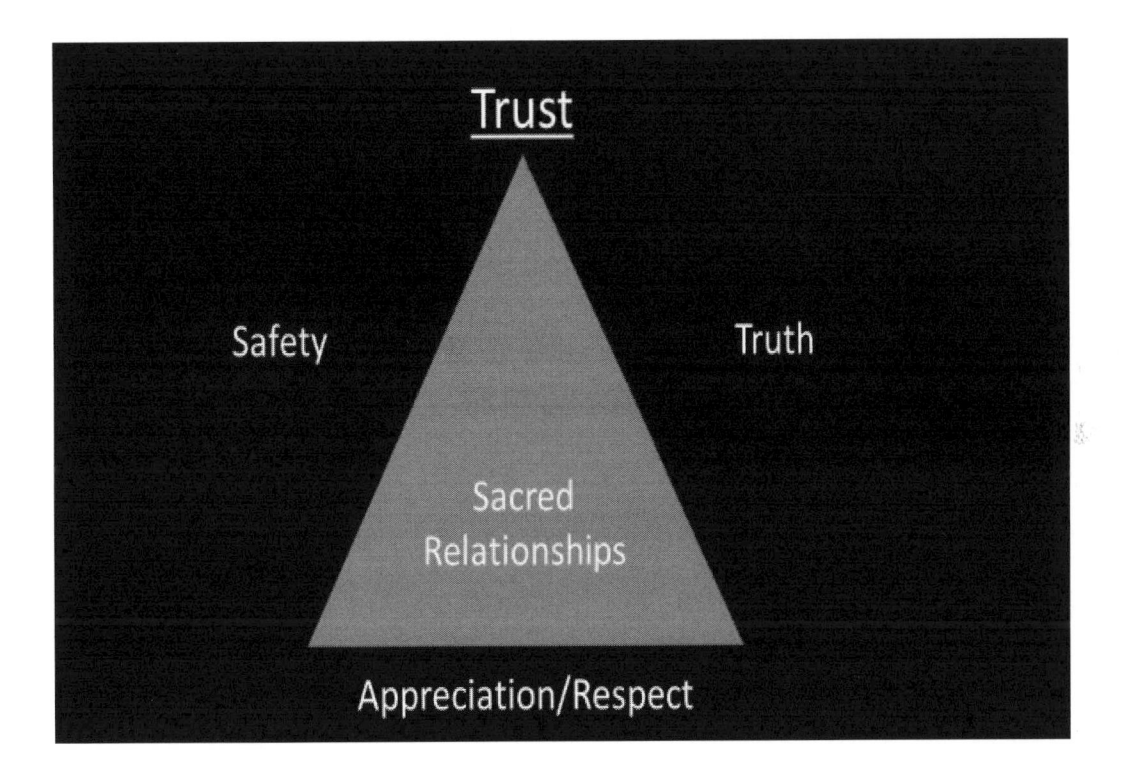

Diagram: A triangle labeled "Sacred Relationships" with "Trust" at the top vertex, "Safety" at the left, "Truth" at the right, and "Appreciation/Respect" at the base.

Appreciation is as important to relationship as respect or trust. If you don't appreciate what I bring to the relationship, I will find someone who will.

"Often when we experience "being in love" (which can be a microcosm of real love) we are so frightened that we eventually begin to find flaws in our partners or friends in order to justify moving from trust to distrust." (Michael Mirdad, *Creating Fulfilling Relationships*)

Building Trust

As you move into the space of the relationship together we might suggest that you take time to define what are the intentions and desires you are bringing into form. Is it about redefining what it means to love on a deeper level? Is it about healing traumas of this and other lifetimes? Is it about supporting each other in our growth and understanding? It may be all of these and more. We only suggest is that you look beneath the surface of your personal desires and romantic fantasies and explore what the deeper meaning of the encounter may be about.

Too often we allow the surface image of our encounters with others obscure the greater possibilities and reasons for our coming together. There are no chance encounters. This is someone with a gift for your soul if you are willing to remove the layers of protection that are preventing this treasure from being revealed.

Along with this, we might suggest that you set aside uninterrupted time for exploration of the deeper mysteries of your life together. If this is a dance worth learning, it behooves you to become familiar with all of the intricacies of the steps before stepping into the spotlight together. Too often partners are caught up in the immediacy of the desire for fulfillment and they fail to prepare for the things that make that possible. If a firm foundation of trust is established, all will flow in divine order.

So how might you go about allowing this to take place? We might suggest that you spend time getting to know each other at an experiential level. The more you are able to share the experiences of your life and what they taught you, the more the other will know of the real you and how you are likely to show up in their lives.

Since the best predictor of future behavior is past behavior, how have you responded in the past or what did you learn that might make this different? This is a process of building the bridge of connection that will allow you to come together at a higher level of experience.

Certainly, the openness and honesty of your conversations will enhance the feelings of connection that will lead to trust. If one can honestly look at their experiences and unbiasly own their stumbles and course corrections, there is a higher likelihood that they will continue on this path of growth. Those who continue to rationalize, make excuses, and come from a victim mentality are unlikely to be ready for the process of Hieros Gamos. This requires that both participants lay bare their souls and their journey to the other because in doing so it releases them from those experiences, allows their completion, and begins the healing journey together.

If truth is not the foundation for a relationship, there will forever be an instability that will cause shakiness in the structure. Trust is built upon inner knowing that whatever occurs, you have not only each other's back, but are committed to processing the challenges of life together. Until you have laid the groundwork for this to occur, you will be unable to find the door that reveals the hidden staircase to divine union.

It behooves you to spend the time in meaningful exploration of not only the motivations, but the abilities of both partners to embark upon this grand adventure together. You might liken it to an ascent up a mountain tethered together. Both must be equipped and confident in the integrity and abilities of the other to assure that they will arrive safely at their destination. Continue to spend the time and energy preparing for the adventure and you will have many "ah ha" moments that will tell you that you are on the right track and ready for the ascent.

Your feelings of connection to the other are significantly enhanced every time you open the door of your heart and give them a peek inside. The deepest longings for fulfillment are facilitated each time you loosen the grip on your personal experiences and make them shared experiences. Now this is not to say that there is nothing that belongs exclusively to you. In fact, you still own all of your thoughts, words and deeds, but it is when they are open to the view of your intimate partner that you begin the process of merging into the arena of sacred relationship.

If it is only God that knows and understands the musings of your inner self, how much more connected does it make your intimate partner when you give them entrance? By allowing all of your secret longings, hopes, and deeds to fall under the scrutiny of the beloved, you give them the deepest gift of your trust.

Now this is not to say that you must bare your soul to everyone who knocks on the door to your heart. However, in the intimacy of a sacred relationship, it is as if each becomes an extension of the other. Without the assurance that the other honors this trust as they do their own fidelity, this would not be possible.

So how do you go about developing trust? We might say again that past action is always the best predictor of future action. If someone has an unblemished track record of integrity and truthfulness, it might be expected that this will continue to be the case. But what if you do not have this experience, or what if the circumstances have altered that might make this supposition less certain? We might suggest that trust is a mountain to be traversed together. It takes practice in navigating the seemingly insignificant terrain to build up the muscles of confidence in the other so you will feel comfortable risking your heart in the more perilous climbs.

As you continue to grow in love and trust together you will be challenged increasingly to explore even greater depths of experience that will give you the confidence that this person is beginning to value your wellbeing as much as they do their own. You will also observe how they treat themselves. Do they take foolish chances or make risky moves that indicate perhaps they are not as well-grounded or respectful of their own health and well-being? Are they overly cautious or fearful, which might indicate that perhaps they have not come to terms with their own faith in themselves or others?

Before you give your heart to another for safekeeping, you might wish to observe how they treat themselves and those around them. Are you comfortable in this space upon which all else will be built, or does there require further scaffolding to be built before you will feel safe? The bridge of trust must be securely in place before embarking on the journey into the divine realms together. However once in there, you are able to see the face of God reflected in your beloved's eyes.
Mary Anna

Ways to Cultivate Trust in a Relationship by Dr. John Gottman

1. **Be Loyal** - Trust will be improbable, if not impossible, if the relationship brings with it a history of infidelity. A relationship shrouded with adulterous beginnings, is destined to fail. A relationship with secrets is also destined for failure. If you have infidelities in your past, it doesn't mean that you are unworthy of trust. If you hide them, it does.

2. **Build Self-Esteem and Confidence** - Building confidence in the relationship itself is important, but it is just as important to build your partner's confidence in him/herself. Taking the time to compliment your partner, especially in front of others, shows you are willing to go out on a limb for him/her. Showing an interest in your partner's hobbies or interests says, "you mean more to me than anyone else." This cultivates trust. It eliminates the doubt that comes with superficiality. It expresses clearly that you are not the center of your own universe. It bridges the gap between feeling and knowing. With adequate confidence, a person is freer to trust not only him/herself, but to trust you. Trust allows you to give freely, without expectations for something in return.

3. **Forgive** - Forgiveness builds insurmountable trust. Do you say you can forgive but you cannot forget? What a wicked dart the un-forgetful mind throws at the inner sanctity of trust. Harbored resentment, grudges, and other negative emotions of the same ilk only serve dis-allusion and skepticism. Retaliation, vengeance, and expectations are their byproduct. If you want someone to trust you, you need to leave bad memories at the door mat. Once an apology is made, accept it. If you say you accept it, then you must live out that acceptance. Otherwise, you will not be trusted. Just as "forgiveness is the fragrance of dew the violet spreads on the heel that crushes it" (unknown), trust is knowing that forgiveness is as certain as rain or sunshine. That doesn't mean you are free to act out and then expect blind forgiveness. It means genuine repentance should be met with genuine acceptance of the repentant, leaving you both free to move past the pain of the circumstances.

4. **Propose** - In early Judaism, a man could marry by sex with a virgin. The act of submission by a woman or man said, in effect, "I Do." In 2800 B.C.E., a ring was used to symbolize a binding partnership. The advent of the diamond engagement ring wasn't until the 1500's. But with or without the sex, the ring, or the paper license to remind you of the day of your nuptials, marriage is actually nothing more than an act of trust. Some might argue that staying together without the ink on the page actually shows more trust than the nuptials do. But the point here is that committing to stay together cultivates trust. The wedding vows were carefully written to carry the message of a binding trust – "in sickness and in health;" "for better or for worse;" "til' death do us part." What a splendid way to cultivate trust in your partner. When you propose marriage or say, "I Do," you are saying to your mate, "you can trust me to be there for you."

5. **Stand Up and Stand For, Don't Just Stand By** - Life throws punches. That is not mere chance, it is fact. Will you stand by your partner when the punches are thrown? Or will you criticize and debunk, leaving them to manage the ravaging waves alone. This form of trust applies analogously to friendships which pre-existed the relationship. If you move into a new relationship and shelter your mate from friends and family, you will breed distrust. If you go out of your way to ensure your partner feels included, rather than excluded, you will build respect and trust. This says to your partner, "you are good enough for my friends." Guard against making unproductive comments to your friends about your partner. Ultimately, whether stated in humor or bachelor crass, the emotional intelligence of the one who trusts you will home in on it. And he/she will not trust you any longer.

6. **Toe the Line** - That old adage that 'trust is earned' is true! You might begin with a clean slate and a blind trust, believing that you have made the choice to trust until someone gives you a reason not to, but ultimately you will be given a reason. Only perfect people won't and there aren't any of those. It takes time to build trust and until that foundation is established, you will be operating blindly on gut instinct and your own sense of knowing. How you react to the dismantling of trust's a Time bomb is critical to maintaining trust in the future. Once an act of distrust occurs, communication is critical. You must explain yourself and you must do it with the kind of sincerity and openness that counter-acts the act of distrust. You must explain your position with compassion, understanding the impact of your crime. An apology will not help you here, but a heartfelt explanation may save you. Admit your insecurities or doubts. This means searching yourself, and that means caring enough about your partner to search yourself!

7. **Walk the Walk** - This should probably be number one on the to-do list for trust. If you say A, then do B, you are not inviting trust. It is equally as bad to say you will do something and then not follow through with it. The consummate excuse maker will only get by a couple of times before trust begins to erode. If you say you will do something, it's simple - just do it. Make yourself trustworthy. In the same vein, it is important to do things for your partner without being asked or told to. Silence on a matter doesn't breed trust any better than excuse making does. Your silence will not go un-noticed when it is perceived that you should step up to the plate but are conveniently quiet on the subject. If you cannot or will not step up to the plate, then you should at least say why you cannot or will not.

Truth

In their book, **The Magdalene Manuscript, The Alchemy of Horus and The Sex Magic of Isis,** Tom Kenyon and Judy Sion talk about the importance of sharing our truth in Sacred Relationships. *"To go out on a limb is to speak the truth, facing the possibility that the other one may not be able to give you what you want. Relationships are rather like poker games with everyone bluffing about who has the higher cards. When you go into Sacred Relationship, all of the cards are laid on the table for each to see. Whatever arises, it is simply put on the table because the clarity of two people looking at the cards allows for the possibility of transformation."*

"This type of relationship demands utmost honesty, both with oneself and one's partner. Without it the Alchemy of Relationship cannot exist. For those in Sacred Relationship it is a call to presence. It is a time to be radically honest and for both partners to express their true feelings no matter how embarrassing or scary they may be. Psychological honesty results in psychological insight. And with insight there is hope for awareness and with awareness there can be change."

Perhaps the greatest commitment we can make to another is "I pledge you my truth".

Laying the Groundwork for Sacred Partnerships

If your intention is to live a life of divine service, we have a few suggestions. First, be aware that many around you may not be at that same level of growth. Expect that those who have not come to the higher level of mastery and understanding will self-select and remove themselves. Such is the spiritual evolutionary process.

Now this is not to say that you should keep your mouth shut as to your real beliefs and feelings, though this is always an option. We might suggest that perhaps your soul is in fact guiding you to a calmer place in the stream where others who share your elevated perspective will congregate.

Second, as Yeshua demonstrated with his inner circle, there are those who are ready for the deeper truths and those who are not. You will know who can be trusted with this knowledge and who have not completed the fundamental learning that would enable them to step up to this to the next level. Not discrimination but discernment.

We would caution you to refrain from any sort of elitism in the process. This is a natural progression, and many must heal the wounds in their lives before they will be able to see the next steps. Your greatest service will be to assist them in that healing to allow them to move forward.

Once you have made the decision to make this your life's purpose, your mission is to remove all the impediments that stand in your way of achievement. Are you strongly tied to a location? Do family responsibilities restrict your movement? How about monetary resources? All of these are valid considerations and may be the lessons you need to master for integration of the Christ Light into form. Not obstacles, but opportunities for growth.

Next we might ask you what this might do to your relationships. What would happen if you were to see yourself as a Christed being? What effect would that have on those around you? Would others applaud your achievement or shrink away, knowing that they do not measure up to that same standard? How would you feel if that were to happen? Would this cause you to abandon the quest or inspire you to help lift them up at your side? These are serious questions that must be considered if you are to make the transition into elevated consciousness. It is like making sure the parachute is in working order before jumping out of the plane.

Now this quest for divine consciousness does not require that you become perfect before beginning. The only requirement is the intention to move towards this goal and to apply this overriding purpose in every aspect of your life. If you have God with you in every decision, how can you lose your way? If you choose to include God in all of your conversations, how can they be anything but holy? If you see through the eyes of God in every aspect of your life you will always Know the right choice and be able to skim the waters of turbulence while others flail against the current. So, what is your commitment to life?

The first step toward the exalted experience of Hieros Gamos, the divine marriage of masculine and feminine, is to have partners who are equally committed to the task. To have one who is headed in a different direction means that they are unevenly yoked and will be forever pulling against each other. What is your deeper commitment? How about your partner? Now this is not to say that they both must be at the same level of understanding; only that they must be headed in the same direction.

Are both willing to help each other heal and grow together in loving, supportive ways? This is the groundwork for sacred partnerships. The intimacy of the journey will bring up all of the unhealed parts we attempt to hide from the world. Without the sanctity and safety of this soul commitment, there will not be a safe space for healing. Think of the previous example of jumping out of a plane with a parachute...together. Hold your partner firmly so that they feel your heart beating close and the protection of your arms around them so they will be able to let go of the fear of the unknown peril and dissolve into the love of the moment. This moment becomes the eternity of souls united in the embrace of the beloved which is the union with God. This is the path to knowing God through the embrace of the divine found in the beloved's arms. This is bliss. We wish you bliss,

Mary Anna

Penny's thoughts:

I have been visiting family for a few days in California which gives me an opportunity for testing what it is like to live as a Christed being. Sometimes family gatherings are mine fields for many, as we can easily trigger childhood issues that were left unresolved. I have found it interesting to observe how these are playing out in my family of origin, my children, grandchildren and great-grandchildren. I decided to begin by seeing all of the past dramas as illusion and intended that our journey together would be a demonstration of loving awareness.

I was careful to greet each person lovingly, making sure I let each one know how happy I was to be with them and how much I loved and had missed them. There was no need to rehash past dramas. I gave each the opportunity to be and feel heard with understanding and not judgment. Where appropriate, when asked, I offered suggestions as to how they might see something in a different light or try a different approach when dealing with situations in their lives. I made it a point to listen carefully to what was going for them and gave encouragement to situations and events that were of a positive nature.

I carefully chose words that reflected a positive vibration to express feelings clearly and respectfully and refused to buy into conversations about things that were less than respectful and loving. Negative, conversations that headed in a degrading or demeaning direction were quickly cut off by stating that "That has not been my experience." This is usually all that is necessary to redirect conversations in a positive direction. It is interesting how quickly gossip can be stopped when someone refuses to listen or respond to third-party experiences.

Be Love

We understand that moving into these higher dimensions of thought may not come easy at first. Ingrained patterns are difficult to change but not impossible. We would like to give you a few examples of how this might be implemented in your lives:

First, do not believe that those around you have not been feeling the same promptings even though they might not have voiced it. Assume that all are traveling in the light as well. Many times, it takes only an affirmation from others that they are heard and understood to foster growth.

Second, if loving energy is the field where you choose to engage with all, do not be afraid to make that your chosen vocabulary. Many times, those around you are searching for the words to use in this "new" way of being. Perhaps you can guide them just by the words you choose and the ideas you are able to slip in. Words have power and by choosing your words carefully, you set intentions as well as create the environment for understanding.

Do not be afraid of "coming out" with your intentions to find more loving ways of being on earth. Many are having similar inclinations but are unsure how to express themselves in doing so. You might jokingly consider yourselves an army of "lovers" bent on overtaking the world. Just making such a statement will alter the tenor of your interaction with those around you. Lead by example.

Your intimate relationships are where your intentions come into form. While professing one's love for another can be intimidating to some if they are not similarly committed, it might take on a different meaning if you were love personified. The more you express your love and appreciation to those in your circle of intimates, the less scary this will become. If you surround yourself in a culture of those who are able to give and share love freely, this will become obvious and second nature to all.

So how does one act in a culture of loving energy. Foremost, we might suggest is that there is an innate caring for those around you. While not elevating them above you, there is an intense feeling that you wish for them to experience all of the goodness and happiness life has to offer. This takes an advanced realization that this in no way detracts from what you experience, but in fact quite the opposite for it raises the energetic vibration of the interaction for all.

Along with this is the intention that both of your experiences be as rich and fulfilling as they can be because of the energy each will intend to make it so. Heightened sensual experiences come about because the partners are fully present with each other and part of the process and not just "phoning it in". If you wish to have a life filled with wonder and joy, it requires that you be fully engaged, with all of your senses and chakra centers fully open, attuned, and ready. Allow the other to step into the new garment of love you are preparing for them.

We might suggest that you set aside previous assumptions. If you went into each interaction oblivious as to what the other person might possess in the way of gifts, abilities, and talents as well as baggage of every kind, how might it change your attitude? Allow the new, evolved, loving face of the other emerge without the baggage of old traumas and encounters being brought to the forefront. Assume that every day brings a fresh start and new adventure waiting to be fulfilled. Frequently we fall back into old patterns because it is too difficult to extricate ourselves from the negative images others hold onto us as we processed the lessons of our life. Let go of all previous images and be willing to hold each other in new garments of loving energy and you will do much to create that reality.

And finally, allow relationships to proceed at their own pace, and the form will reveal itself. You do not have to categorize your interactions with others as romantic, fraternal, business or others just because that is the way it initially presented. For those to which you feel an energetic attraction, allow the discovery of the purpose to present itself slowly as you draw from each other at a soul level the gifts you came together to exchange. We are all gifts to each other for our growth and understanding. We are also blank slates to write upon our love letters to the divine expressed in the intimacy of our relationships. Embrace those in your life who give you this opportunity for divine encounters and BE the love you wish to receive from others. You are God's loving gift to the world...
Mary Anna

Penny's thoughts:

Mary Anna's message got me thinking about the different types of loving relationships I have in my life. After my husband died and I moved to Sedona, I was essentially starting from scratch because no one knew me, or my history and I did not know them. I could recreate myself in any image I wished. I decided to be love.

When I first attended Unity of Sedona here it was like walking into a family reunion. Though I had never met these people in this lifetime, it was as if we knew each other on a soul level. I have come to believe that this is indeed a soul group that has traveled together for many lifetimes, but that is another story detailed in my book, *Soul Weaving*. I have continued to grow within this family of choice in many loving ways. This is not to say that we have had no differences of opinion; quite the contrary. However, we are committed to growing together and this requires being mirrors and holding each other in love, not judgment, until we "get" the lesson.

A much-loved congregant recently passed at age 90. Her legacy will be shared by many who turned out to honor this beautiful, vibrant soul who inspired us all to loving more profoundly. Her much repeated motto was *"You have to get up, dress up, and show up, because someone out there needs your love"*. She did every day and was love expressed in form.

I had never had men friends before who were not romantic partners or partners of my friends. I have learned that most of the men in my life are there to show me the face of love expressed in many forms. In this community I have men and women hug me every day and tell me they love me, and I respond in kind. I have never felt so much loving energy shared spontaneously and unflinchingly. Very little of it is sexual attraction. It is really about respect, appreciating and caring on such a deep level that it can only be called love or agape. I think that is what Mary Anna is talking about, when she talks about allowing the form to reveal itself.

Understanding our Complimentary Nature

We all have attributes of both the masculine and feminine, regardless of our gender. Our challenge is balance and integration.

Your Feminine Aspect

SHE in you is the 'Human Being". One of the major potent gifts of the Feminine is the ability to be – to be open to receive. HER power is in HER willingness and ability to be vulnerable.

SHE is open to receive the natural gifts, creativity, inspiration, intuition and guidance of your Soul.

The Feminine qualities are also associated with being nurturing, loving, expansive, flowing, intuitive, boundary-less, earth connected, life-birthing, affirming, gentle, and creative. SHE trusts the process and natural cycles of life. SHE is cooperative, emotionally available, relational, inclusive, compassionate, complimentary, empowering, a healing conduit and a visionary.

Ironically, the most important Feminine Power is the ability to be vulnerable – to be open.

Your Masculine Aspect

HE is the "Doer… the "Human Doing" HE protects the wall that you created and went out onto the battlefield of your life.

HE generates the ability to give, provide, protect and do. HE is that aspect of you that makes things happen and manifest in the world.

Some of HIS gifts and abilities in your life may be qualities such as being structured, focused, goal-oriented, competitive, driven, grounded, stable, dependable, protecting, exploring, conquering, logical, controlling and self- contained. These give him the ability to bring the creative inspirations of your Feminine into form.

The literal mind is one of the tools of the Masculine. In addition, he may be power and control seeking and hard-working which makes HIM the perfect producer of your Soul's expressions in the world.

Enocha Rangita Ryan

Preparing for a Loving Partnership

The encounters you have with all around you are opportunities for developing your abilities to lovingly engage with an intimate partner on a deeper level. In such a partnership, you will reveal yourself on such a transparent level that it is imperative that love be something that is innately a part of your being and not just a frock that you don for the occasion. When we say BE love it means just that – it becomes a vibration that acts like a filter through which all actions and intentions flow. It is part of your being and who you are. Everyone you come into contact with will feel the love that you are.

So how do you hold this loving vibration when stressed with the challenges of your life? We first might suggest that you begin each day in prayer and meditation. Connection daily with this inner source of inspiration and guidance helps with the "preventive maintenance" your soul requires to keep everything on track and clearly and optimally functioning. Consider it a spiritual recalibration where intentions are set, and misalignments are corrected. Take time throughout the day to check in and see if there is a need for course corrections or to give yourself a "high five" because things are going even better than you thought.

It is helpful to check with those of your inner circle who love you in the deeper sense of the word. Those with "security clearance" to this level of intimacy should be emotionally clear and advanced enough that they are looking out for your back and have only your best interest at heart, regardless of how it impacts them. Though all may not yet be masters at this level of loving friendship, this should at least be the guidelines for those you hold in this role of trusted intimate. As you learn these skills together and expand your friendship, you will be developing important "love muscles" that will serve you well in deeper intimate relationships.

As you have learned of the three types of relationships with God, self and others, the one with self is frequently the most difficult to come to terms with. When we see ourselves as less than loveable and flawed, rather than a work in progress, we create a mental image that projects to the world for others to receive. If you want to be seen as loveable to others, you must think yourself worthy of that image. Are your "flaws" the things that define you or merely blemishes that are in the process of healing and give you character as you move out of your emotional adolescence?

It is unrealistic to think that we can develop into emotionally balanced, loving individuals without going through the fires that temper us on the way. Being able to embrace these lessons, learn and grow from them, and share the cautionary tale with others is the gift of growth and leadership. Allow yourself to bless both the challenges as well as the triumphs for these are the merit badges that make you most trusted and admired in the arena of emotional service to each other. The more you are able to share your process and growth with each other on an intimate scale, the easier it will become to develop that level of intimacy with a partner with whom you will share the Hieros Gamos.

True intimacy requires that we share the depth of our soul with the other. Anything less leaves exposed the veils we hide behind that obscure our real self. If you wish to deeply know another, you must be willing to reveal that level of intimacy within yourself. That includes your deepest fears, motivations, and insecurities. As you lay bare your heart to another, you open that door and invite them into your own. This is the return to the divine, hand in hand with the beloved. We wish you love...

Mary Anna

Penny's thoughts:

I had a lot to learn about the breadth of loving relationships after my husband died. I had spent my former life in the structure of marriage and family. My loving relationships seemed to grow in and around that arena. Any friendships with men were usually in conjunction with their wives and were more superficial in nature. Women in my circle of friends shared concerns with family and community but seldom touched the honesty and depth I was to later experience. This was a time of preserving an image of wholeness, rather than addressing the things that were preventing it. No wonder the seventies were a time of revolution and rebellion. It was evident something was not working correctly, and we had missed a critical turn on the path.

After my husband, Gordon, passed I had an opportunity to realize the tremendous comfort and growth in a circle of conscious women. These women were real and weren't afraid of expressing their struggles and their insights with sisters on the path. I became aware that this was not a competition, but a shared journey into awareness. I felt the love that they had for me and was able to reflect it back to them in true appreciation for what it was teaching me.

I really ramped up the process when I came to Sedona. My friend, Don offered to rent me a room in his house to see if I liked it. I could continue to sit on the sofa in Albuquerque or move to Sedona??? I moved everything I could fit into my little Kia and have not looked back. It has been an amazing journey of discovering, blending, embracing the divine, in all aspects of my life.

I was to discover the joy and value of soul brothers and how we are able to work together in incredibly deep and meaningful ways, when issues around sexual attraction are not muddying up the process. I deeply appreciate the care, love, respect, honesty, and trust they share with me daily, as we move together through this process of awareness and growth. Our dance of masculine and feminine, uncolored by gender, has been revealing to us all allowing us to embrace aspects of our divine selves in mutually supportive ways. By reflecting our observances from our spot on the "elephant" (Reference the fable of the blind men describing an elephant from their limited perception and experience) we are gradually piecing together a greater vision of the whole and our own part in the divine plan.

I have learned the value of daily prayer and meditation in keeping me focused and aware. It is easy to get sidetracked with the business and challenges that we encounter on a daily basis, without this recalibration process. I begin my morning with Michael Mirdad's version of the Lord's Prayer you will find in the Endnotes[iii]. Kathleen McGowan in her book *Source of All Miracles* refers to the seven parts of the Lord's Prayer as correlating to the petals in the center of the Labyrinth. I believe it also correlates with rebalancing the seven chakras. By feeling deeply into these affirmations, I set the tone for my meditation and my day.

I personally find it more effective to use this as a time of contemplation and meditation. If I find my mind wandering in meditation, as it is apt to do, I take this as a sign that I need to go deeper into this issue, to get out of my own way, and objectively look at it from this elevated perspective. As an experienced dowser of many years, I frequently take a pendulum into my meditation and read the energy with my eyes closed during the process to help guide me in the assessing of alternatives. Probably not how others do it, but this is something that I am guided to do and works well for me.

I am most appreciative and grateful for the many ways love is presenting its many faces in my life and am committed to opening up to this in ever-increasing ways with all on this divine journey together.

Walking a Common Path

If you feel that your connection with the divine is a bit tenuous, we have a few suggestions:

First, do you consider yourself worthy of the process? In order to believe that you are indeed an aspect of your divine self, you must be able to see yourself as being part of that mystery. If this is not presently the case, what veils might you remove that will allow that divine vision to expose itself? Is it because you are not "perfect" in your expression in life? What makes you believe that perfection is necessary to aspire to divinity? If in fact you had achieved perfection, would you still be here in third-dimensional experience? You might wish to reconsider your definition of divinity to include those who are committed to the path and working towards that end. One foot in front of the other...

Second, is your vision of others contingent upon how well they measure up to your exacting standards? What can you do to hold this mirror for them so that they also will be able to focus on the divine aspirations that will help make this so? Do you hold others to a different standard from yourself or are you willing to assist where necessary to help each other over the potholes in life, compassionately and caringly?

What attributes do you consider to be of a divine nature? Is it about charity to others or removing the log from your own eye? Is it a divine attribute to focus on self-realization as a way to make the world a better place? Certainly, charity must begin at home as must loving awareness. Begin to mirror this to each other and you step into the divine blueprint.

The walk with the divine aspects of your beloved must certainly be one of gentleness. If you treat their heart with the same loving kindness that you do your own, how could it be otherwise? It is when we see the other as differently aligned from the common purpose, which is the sacred relationship, that we move further away from this reality. You might wish to create a symbol or a phrase that represents for you both this intention. You are mirrors for each other to remind your beloved that perhaps you are straying off this agreed upon path. By catching yourself and your partner when your intentions stray from the mutual intention, you can make the course corrections together.

Now this is not to say that you must agree about everything. You are there to learn and grow together. Rather, it is a commitment to hear and see each other respectfully and forgo judgment as you mutually discuss how something is affecting you. Being able to see through the eyes of the beloved will help you to find a common path together that helps both grow in the process. You may not come to the same conclusion, but if each feels honored and heard, there is respect built into the process. Feeling safe enough to speak honestly about your process builds a foundation of trust and appreciation upon which all love relationships must have to grow and thrive.

Allow your heart to open wide enough to welcome in this, sometimes challenging, participant in your own growth and awakening and you will find yourselves moving deeper into the heart of love. Be love...
Mary Anna

Penny's thoughts:

It occurs to me that you do not have to have a current beloved to practice this process. In fact, it might be helpful to build up some "muscles" in this area before moving into a significant romantic relationship.

I have been blessed to share a house with conscious men over the last few years and it has been quite a learning and growing experience for us all. Though we are all quite different, we have developed such a loving, respectful, trusting, honest relationship that there is virtually nothing we cannot discuss. We do use each other as sounding boards to see if we are operating in a loving, egoless state, or if there is a hidden agenda behind our actions that we may be missing. Many times, those who know us best can see things that we are reluctant to admit to ourselves.

I believe that the cornerstone to this, as Mary Anna has stated, is trust and appreciation. Given the birds-eye view of some of our relationship experiences we have shared with each other that seems to be the most important indicator as to whether they continue to grow or drop away.

I see the divinity emerging in my soul brothers and we continue to hold that mirror unflinchingly for each other, congratulating our triumphs, and helping each other over the rough spots. We are blessed because we are willing to share this path together in loving respect and appreciation. Namaste my brothers.

Ah Ha Moments

The tenuous veil between dimensions is separating you from your soul essence because you have not been willing to embrace that part of your being. Your continued downgrading of your beliefs that you are anything less than an aspect of your divine Creator, prevents this from manifesting in form. As you believe, you create that reality.

What would happen if all believed they were an aspect of the divine, in third-dimensional expression? How different might be their experience? If you were to believe that you are part of the family of God, as are all around you, how might that alter your experience in this world? If you recognize your partner as also part of this divine lineage, would it alter how you perceive your actions together?

So, what does it mean to embrace your divinity? We might suggest that you begin by seeing things as God might see them. Is your vision of God judgmental or forgiving? If you are to see the divinity in your partner, how might you look at their "faults" as opportunities to administer the healing balm of love in order to foster growth and understanding? What do they do that "presses your buttons" because it triggers unhealed parts of yourself? Is it perhaps because you are still experiencing judgment and criticism rather than looking for ways to lovingly work together in divine partnership to resolve any imbalance? Our partners are there to help us see the divine path of love and help us to make course corrections by shining the light on the things that separate us from our divine nature. We make peace with them and the world around us when we no longer see our differences as detriments but look upon them as opportunities for growth in understanding.

So, what is to be gained by focusing on the "shortcomings" of the other? Do we feel more superior or empathetic if we know that our partners have work to do in an area that we have mastered? Or do we look at it as an opportunity to gently and lovingly guide them on a common path of discovery? The higher you step on the vibrational ladder, the greater the opportunity for course corrections and adjustment in concert with your beloved. Do not become overly concerned with the "hows", just allow the flow of divine love to help lift you over the rough spots. If you continually come back to "What is the most loving choice I can make right now?", you will be able to help each other through the fog of indecision.

Do not be surprised if the decision to join in a process of Hieros Gamos does not bring up a number of difficult challenges for you. When you step into this higher vibrational field, all of the things that do not resonate here will become obstacles on the path. It is as if you are entering graduate school of the heart. It is incumbent upon you to tackle the harder courses in order to move into a higher level of understanding. The partner you have chosen for this process has their own courses of mastery to share as well. The good part is that you have both completed all of the undergraduate course work, made your early missteps, and learned from the curriculum. It is more of a process of coordination and recalibration of your emotions to bring the parts into resonance.

The experiences of your life have prepared you for the exact moment of recognition that this is the event you have been waiting for. All of the pieces fit and you both realize that all is coming together in divine recognition. It is the "Ah Ha" moment where anticipation crosses into fulfillment that you Know that finally all of the preliminary work is about to pay off. Finally, you are ready to allow the magic to unfold. Let the adventure begin...
Mary Anna

Penny's Thoughts:

Yesterday brought a lot to the surface to be healed between my housemate and myself. This has been a particularly stressful time in our lives with many moving parts as we both transition into new phases of our lives. It has been a pattern for me to be a sounding board for him and sit patiently while he downloads his story before I respond. This allows him to keep his focus and air his "stuff" but gives me little opportunity to share my feedback and insights during the process. By the time he is through, I have usually lost my train of thought or have given up, tuned out, and moved on to other things. He may feel heard, but I certainly have not! Plus, we miss the opportunity to benefit from the other's wisdom and perspective. Though there is a deep love and respect, it is not an equal partnership, or one that facilitates growth or understanding. He always comes back and apologizes, but the teachable moment for both is lost. Fortunately, we both realize that these are patterns we need to work on that will influence how we handle all of the intimate relationships in our lives.

Part of the problem is that we do not have uninterrupted time together to discuss the situation and to communicate on a deeper level how the challenges in our lives are affecting us. The cell phone is a constant interruption and distractions that breaks the train of thought. The underlying feeling is that whatever we are discussing is of lesser importance than the incoming call or text. He is so busy multitasking and moving from one commitment to the next that we do not set aside quality time together to really hear what the other is saying and, more importantly, the underlying feelings around that. We tend to project what the other's reactions and thoughts might be rather than checking to see if these have grown or changed through our experiences.

We may think we know each other well, but in fact, we only scratch the surface and know a portion of the other, but by no means the depth and breadth of what and who we really are all about. Perhaps our dance together is to perfect our communication skills so that we are able to use these to create the intimate partnerships we both want in our lives.

I printed out the above and left it for him to read. It brought up many things for both of us, but he totally got it. I also realized my complicity in this and how I had allowed this disempowering behavior to dictate the structure of our relationship. We both agreed that it was not healthy and honoring of each other and had created habits we did not want to take into other relationships.

We began a new pattern of being together. We silenced cell phones and other detractors when we are talking together. We take turns sharing and intentionally focus on what the other is saying rather than jumping ahead to our response or judgment. While we have not resorted to mirroring the exact words the other has said, that would certainly be an option if we feel we are slipping back into old habits. There is a great deal of respect and appreciation here and we each find opportunities to convey that to the other through our interaction and conversation rather than continually pointing out the things the other does that might annoy us. By both of us bringing our "A game" to the relationship and making the course corrections we need, we help polish our abilities that will allow us to create sacred relationships in all areas of our lives. This is a lot more fun!

Deepening Experiences of Love

Today I would like to talk about different kinds of love. While you may think of love being between a man and a woman, this only begins to touch the surface of the complex expression of love being experienced in your world. We are brought into this world into the loving arms of a mother and father. It is here that we begin to experience the love of God being experienced in form. Many do not receive this unconditional love from the beginning and spend much of their lifetime trying to fill this void. That is where loving partnerships can come into play. It is in the loving arms of each other that we are allowed to re-experience this bond linking us back to the Source of our being.

There are many other kinds of loving relationships that help nurture us on the path. As we mature physically we have opportunities to experience the agape love of friendship. Our friends are our soul mates who have incarnated to assist us in remembering the divine qualities that link us with our Creator. It is through the mirrors that they provide that we see our truth and are able to make the course corrections we require for our journey Home.

In adolescence we have the opportunity to begin to experience the first stirrings of the possibilities of deeper love and the intimacy of sexual union. While these are initially fraught with disappointment and moments of illumination, they are preparing us for the deeper mystery of conscious union with the divine.

As our soul journey continues we continue to learn the lessons of mastery of the divine gifts of intimacy. We begin to understand that the more we surrender to our true nature of loving awareness, the easier it is to grasp the brass ring of divine love. This is the path to sacred partnership with the divine.

As we enter the new paradigm of Hieros Gamos, love begins to morph into the full expression of love fully manifested in partnership with the Creator. The gifts that the beloveds bring to the altar of love are the perfected versions of themselves in progress, offered to each other as steppingstones to even greater awareness. It is in these gifts, fully offered, that they will be able to realize the loving state of ecstasy with the Creator.

Now as to how this is manifesting in your world, we would like to say that the first step to this divine awareness is making sure the partners are motivated and conscious. This is not to say that their knowledge must be equal, but that they must be equally committed to each other and the journey together.

They must be willing to set aside previous beliefs and judgments about what the relationship should look like. Gender, age, status are no longer criteria for the process of divine union. There must be instead a commitment to each other and the spiritual growth of themselves as well as the relationship that will hold them together in the turbulent waters ahead. This may take the form of a contractual marriage, but more often not, as the requirements of church and state no longer bind you to the world of form. It is a greater commitment at the level of the soul that is the strength and purpose behind the union.

And finally we would suggest that there is a joy beyond earthly experience that is being birthed when two souls step into their divine natures and fully embrace all of the aspects of the masculine and feminine, fully realized in self and each other in the divine union of Hieros Gamos. This is the gift of the One.

Mary Anna

Attracting Your Energetic Partner

If you feel that you are in this world but not of it, this is essentially so. Around you are those who are struggling in opposition to each other because they have not opened the door to the heart which is the passage to peace and tranquility. We might suggest that your journey will be calmer if you choose to surround yourselves with those who reflect the same level of peace, tranquility, and loving acceptance as you do. If you wish to share an energetic frequency, learn to distance yourselves from those who do not share that vibratory level.

As to how this plays into choosing a romantic partner, we might suggest that while you may be attracted to others who are members of your soul group, there will be one who possesses the energetic wiring to connect in sacred partnership. This will not prevent your learning about discernment from the others, but the one who matches you energetically will be, without question, the best match for you in not only vibration (attraction), but have the missing pieces that will enhance and empower you on your higher path. Those with whom you will have to compromise your goals and desires in order to come together in relationship are not the best match.

As for purpose together, this does not necessarily mean that both must have the same vision. In fact, both may have complementary parts to each other's. Far more important is that the vibrational frequency and level of spiritual mastery should be compatible in order to assure that they will be working together rather than in competition or distance.

Physical attraction is a process of attunement. One feels in the other missing frequencies in their own energetic wiring. While this is beyond the cognitive reckoning of the third-dimensional mentality, it is a significant factor and something that is known in your world as "chemistry". It is the magnetic frequency that draws one to another and begins the dance of love.

Awareness of the attraction is only the beginning. In lower forms of awareness, this may be confused with love, while in fact it is only the invitation to go deeper. Once you have each other's attention, it behooves you to begin exploring the other at a soul level. What are the qualities present or missing in the other that compliments your own? How might you weave them together in the dance of love? What are the motivations and constraints that define the other? Are these compatible with your own? Are the joys you experience in being together worth the struggles that will be required to heal the longings and woundings of the heart?

While this may sound cold and distant, when compared to the distractions of unbridled desire, it is in fact part of the deeper process of loving awareness. It is looking beneath the paint and glitter of emotional lust and ascertaining if this is the soulmate for which we have been searching. It requires sharpening our own perceptions as to who we are and what we not only desire but need at a soul level in order to complete our dance card of experience.

It is strengthening our ability to look into the soul of another and ascertain what is required and how we might achieve it. It is removing the rose-colored glasses of infatuation and seeing clearly if this person is capable and willing to travel together and take the higher path of sacred partnership. Most are not for they have not reached that level of spiritual maturity, but when you have raised your vibration to that frequency, you will magnetize to you those who have a compatible energy.

Allow your preconceived notions of what the ideal relationship should look like and you will attract to you the beloved your soul has called into the dance. Begin to see each other as radiating beings of light and that will be your experience and your reality. This is the promise of your soul...

Mary Anna

The Gift of our Soulmates

In moving toward, a divine relationship there is something we would like to bring your attention to. It is important to see your partner in this quest as an aspect of that state. Now he/she may not appear on the surface to embody this fully, but this is part of the illusion. If you begin to see your partner as an emissary of the divine sent to guide you into that holy union, you will begin to appreciate how this is happening in your life, and you are a divine gift to him/her as well.

The excitement begins when we begin to unwrap the gifts we have for each other. On the surface we may be thinking "Now why would God want me to have this? It is not even my size, shape, color, etc." Exactly! If you are to move forward toward your divine partnership, it is evident that you need to try something different or you would already be there now!

As you scrutinize this gift of unlikely appearance, you might think about what makes it different. If you have always been attracted to "A", what might "B" have to offer your growth and understanding that "A" did not? If you automatically are repulsed by something, what is this triggering in you in the way of compassion to look deeper into your own prejudice? How does looking outside the box help you move into an awareness beyond your comfort zone and expand not only your horizons, but understanding of the greater world calling for your healing? Perhaps this is something you need to address.

As you unwrap the strange gift, you will be triggered to look deeper into your own values, beliefs, and desires. Which are outmoded and ready to be discarded? Which hold up because they are leading you into greater awareness and mastery? How might you use this new opportunity for growth and understanding to help you transcend and grow in compassion and awareness?

Now this is not to say that all gifts are keepers; only that they are worth examining and evaluating for their worthiness for partnership on the divine journey together. If you determine that this partner is indeed worth further scrutiny, what might you do to assure that your journey together is divinely orchestrated? We might suggest that you begin by seeing each other as gifts from God, waiting to be unwrapped. Any imperfections are gifts to you and opportunities to practice compassion and caring on your healing journey together. This is an opportunity for growth and understanding beyond the scope of everyday experience. It is a walk together in the frequency of love and understanding where true healing occurs. You are gifts to each other to enable this to take place.

Few are able to experience this priceless gift because they are unwilling to get past the wrappings that may be tattered and shopworn. They are not willing to continue to delve deeper past the packing and protection to unveil the heart of God within. They are unwilling to allow their own cloaking to be disturbed for fear of exposing themselves at the deeper level. What they do not understand is that this is where the magic of the Hieros Gamos takes place, in the joining and revealing of the heart, unfettered to each other. When all pretense is stripped away, it is two hearts beating as One that create the divine union. This is the gift fully expressed from God.

Mary Anna

Preparing for Divine Partnership

So how do you go about establishing a divine partnership? First we might suggest that an honest discussion must be had with your soulmate to make sure that this is a mutual goal and that both are on the same page. If either has one foot on the dock and another on the boat, this will not be possible.

In this conversation it is important to define and describe what this might look like in its most idealized form. What are your expectations, beliefs and requirements and what are your partner's? Are there unresolved issues for either of you that need to be examined in the process? Do either of you have fears, misgivings, or unhealed wounds that need to be addressed as well? All of these are concerns and challenges that will come up as we grow together in the adventure of ascension to a divine state of being. Now this is not to say that each will be ready for sainthood at the end, but it merely defines the scope so that all are working together in truth and honesty with no hidden agendas.

Next we might suggest that you set aside uninterrupted time to come together to engage at the level of the heart. Fitting pieces in around already crowded schedules seldom gives the time, focus, or priority to allow the magic to unfold. This needs to be a burning desire for each partner for them to take it seriously and make it a priority in their life. They must appreciate the significance of the process and the rewards and be willing to make time and clear their plate in order for the depth of it to unfold.

Now this is not to say that this must be an all-consuming part of your life. However, the more that you engage in the process, it will permeate every aspect of it because you will become the love you wish to see in the world. As you glow in the radiance of fully realized loving partnership, it will be reflected in every aspect of your existence. You might wish to think of yourself as a chrysalis emerging into a butterfly of fully expressed love.

And do not think this will not be fun! Joy is indeed a byproduct of love fully expressed. Imagine the heartfelt joy of merging with someone who sees and appreciates you on the deepest level and you them. Now imagine creating a life with them and others that share and radiate this loving energy to all you encounter. It is a heartfelt embrace with the divine of creation and a dance of beloveds into ecstasy. Now that is joyful.

Mary Anna

The Commitment

The feelings you have for another might be likened to the energetic threads that bind you together. There is a fabric of association that weaves all souls into a matrix of being. Now those of you who have agreed to share a lifetime together have patterns you have come to complete. You might liken this to a cloth of many colors in which other souls incarnate together to weave the pattern.

So how does this play out in the realm, of intimate relationships? We might suggest that there has been agreement before incarnation that predetermines a pattern to be addressed. Now this is not to say that there cannot be a deviation from this for the rule of free will is still in effect; only that this is the blank stage where two are to meet. What transpires thereon is up to the participants to draw on their cellular memory and see if they can elevate this experience to a higher level.

Now that is exactly what is taking place in the process of Hieros Gamos. Both parties have agreed to meet at this time and place to help raise the vibration of the planet and themselves through this experience. There is nothing random about the occurrence for the souls involved have spent many lifetimes together and recognize each other at a soul level. This is in fact a culmination of the loving experience for it reunites soul lovers in physical form.

As to how you begin this process, we might suggest that once you have shared the mental process of recognition and affirmation of attraction, you might wish to connect spiritually through prayer and/or meditation together. Baring your soul requires that you open this portal of experience to create a platform on which to build this soulful relationship. As we have mentioned, this requires that the two come together in equal commitment to the third entity which is the shared relationship with God. It is through this doorway that access is linked with the divine. Anything less is merely a third-dimensional experience.

Along with this commitment to embarking on the journey to Hieros Gamos is the commitment to the other for truth, honesty, protection, and fidelity. If one is to expose themselves in totality to the other, it requires nothing short of full disclosure of not only intent and motivation but anything that might stand in the way so that it can be addressed and healed together. This becomes a commitment to God, through your beloved to act as a surrogate in this divine endeavor. You become agents of the divine in service to each other.

We would also suggest that you make a commitment to each other to set aside uninterrupted time together to be in this loving energy on a regular basis. Many intentions fall by the wayside in a world of distractions without a clear understanding between the partners as to what is important, which is the relationship, and what are third-dimensional distractions that can wait until later. There needs to be a clear understanding beforehand as to what is really an emergency that threatens life and health and what is not.

Once you are in the sacred space you will find that the things that bind you to the exterior world will fall away and you are free to explore the depths of your journey together. To see and be seen clearly and honestly as the reflection of the divine within creates a bond that allows you to enter the pattern of Hieros Gamos together. Your commitment to each other and the process opens the door...

Mary Anna

Divine Intimacy

There is so much interest in your world about the whole subject of sexual intimacy, I would like to discuss that aspect of relationships separately.

First, it is important to know that this beautiful expression of physical love is indeed part of God's plan. Though much has been distorted by different expressions of faith, the fact remains it is through this act of physical union that we find the full expression of our love for God expressed in the form of our beloved. There is nothing sinful or dirty about this however there has been much distortion of the process by those who miss the part about divine union.

Second, we would like to note that it is when the integration of the healed aspects of the lower chakras come into union with the realized aspects of the upper, there is a symphony of completeness that allows the participants to express their divine aspects fully and completely.

As for how this is finding expression in your world…unfortunately too many are so preoccupied with the physical mechanics of sexual expression that they fail to experience the magnificence of love fully realized in the arms and hearts of a true beloved. When this is the culmination of union on all of the levels of experience, it becomes a celebration that extends past the limits of earthly expression and becomes one of exalted bliss. As to how you might experience this bliss, we have a few suggestions:

1. Set aside all demands of the ego and concentrate on being the fullest expression of love in your understanding to your beloved. If each makes the focus of their journey together, a celebration and honoring of the full magnificence of the divine aspects of the other, there leaves little room for third-dimensional illusions.
2. Be there wholly, without distractions in this divine celebration. The more you remove yourself into an altered state and space of loving awareness and joy, the sweeter and deeper will be your experience.
3. You are there to minister to the passions and needs of your partner. Be sensitive to their feelings, hurts, wounds, and emotions because you have taken time to understand these and help heal them together. You are there to apply the healing balm of love to each other and to awaken the full expression of sexually ecstasy without restraint.
4. Take time to build a level of trust, safety, and appreciation between each other so that the joining of the interlocking parts of the whole will feel more like a sacrament of expression of the love you share.
5. Learn to communicate at a soulful level your feelings desires and emotions during the process so that this becomes a deeply shared expression of the adventure together into the heart of love.
6. Express your joy, appreciation, and share your experiences with your beloved so he/she can be even more forthcoming.
7. Look deeply into your lover's eyes and feel the heart connection as two become one flesh and one heart.
8. Linger together and appreciate what has been shared and received and how this has brought you more fully into your divine expression.
9. Know that this has not only brought you closer together into the truth of love, but that you will never wish to settle for less than this peak experience with each other.

The sexual shudder the feminine experiences during deep intimate contact anoints the masculine with the energetic spark that helps him transform his baser instincts into the sublime union of the divine aspects of the masculine and feminine.

This is the full expression of the merging with God in the form of your beloved consummated. We wish you love fully expressed and nothing less.

Much Love, Mary Anna

Becoming One

We would like to talk today about the gifts we share with each other. As you come together with your spiritual and romantic partner, there are many things that you will be able to address and not only heal but empower in each other. The intimacy of Hieros Gamos dissolves the barriers and membranes that separate one from another. It is as if in the physical coming together, there is the genesis of a merged being that embodies the aspects of the two into One.

As for how this might play out in your existence, we might suggest that all awareness is about removing the layers of cloaking that keep us from seeing the magnificence of our divine being. We put up these shields to protect us from our inner knowing until we are ready to address it on a conscious level. Many go through life only operating on the surface level until they are challenged by another to move deeper on the journey. It is the partners to our soul who have the keys to unlock these inner passages and uncover the treasures within.

As you awaken, you will be called to continually delve deeper on this journey of the heart. The simultaneous processing of discovery and revelation of these inner treasures is a joint endeavor when approached together. Once you set aside the masks of the separate self and learn to operate in the context of the Oneness of partnership in the relationship, you will begin to see how the interlocking parts of the whole come together in magnificence.

This is an alchemical process of fusion into the sacred union of Hieros Gamos that has been waiting for expression. It is Oneness that has found expression as two pieces of the heart come together in perfect alignment. It is when each recognizes and honors their unique characteristics that make them the perfect complement of the other that the magic and the process begin. There is a realization that they are not there to conform to the aspects of the other, but to complement them so that the parts will fit together in divine harmony.

As you shift into this expanded awareness of the dance of beloveds, we encourage you to keep in mind that this is all about loving awareness. It is an awareness of each other as a gift from God for your growth and understanding. But more than this, it is an awareness that by coming together with each other in divine order you reflect the essence of God, perfectly manifested as love in the essence of form. This is the promise of divine fulfillment as One.

Mary Anna

Invitation to the Dance

It is in the coming together with our energetic complement in surrender to the greater mystery of love that we come closest to touching the face of God. If you begin to see your partner in this experience as a reflection of the divine, given as a gift to you to help you uncover your own divine nature, you will begin to realize the importance of this process. Allow the distractions of each other's humanness to dissolve into the background and know that there is something greater which is beyond the "logic" of the third-dimensional world taking place.

As to how this might manifest in your life, we might suggest that you begin by assuming an observational stance in the process. If you are willing to step back and be a neutral observer of the dance of the beloveds, you will notice the process of divinity unfolding. As each sheds their protective shell of chrysalis, there is a vulnerability of newly exposed emotions and feelings, wet behind the ears, waiting to be expressed. There is the impulse to withdraw, but an even stronger prompting from the soul that knows that this is the path to God beckoning you forward.

As we become accustomed to being seen in our full radiance by the other, we become emboldened because they are opening up to our scrutiny as well. How good it feels to be seen for who we are without pretense or veiling. We are encouraged to reveal more and to thus emerge slowly and completely until we stand fully exposed, soul to soul with the beloved.

As you come to know each other in every sense of the word, it is important to understand that this is God's gift for your unveiling. There are surprises that await in the process, but only if you remain transparent and fully present will you receive their gifts. Any misunderstandings must be clarified and examined because they only obscure the lessons you came together to experience.

The beauty of the dance together is revealed when both are fully present, healthy, and whole. Anything that prevents that is there for healing. The commitment to this process allows the injured party to submit to the other so that healing can take place. When we reveal to God, in the form of our beloved the hurts and traumas of our life and see the lessons and growth we experienced in each, we become surrogates for the healing presence of God. We are agents of God's love which is the ultimate healer of all pain and discomfort.

Being able to share this gift with our beloved elevates our experience together as something holy and sacred. This will define your experience if you keep this perspective in your interaction. You are the arms of God embracing your beloved. Be love.

Mary Anna

The Dance of Beloveds

You will notice different sensations in your physical body as you come into resonance with your divine partner. This is an attunement process of adjusting polarities much as connecting the positive and negative cables on a car. It is two bodies learning to move as one in a well-rehearsed dance to the symphony of life. Initially there may be some stepping on toes until the steps become imprinted in your cellular memory. You will want to start slowly as you become accustomed to the new vibration of the sacred journey together.

Repeated stumbling by one partner usually means that there is dissonance on some level that must be adjusted before the process can be reengaged. So how do you deal with chronic clumsiness in the dance of love? We might suggest that your time would be well spent in honest communication, exploring the feelings and emotional triggers the situation brings up. This is your soul's gift brought into your awareness for transformation and healing. You have drawn to you the perfect balm, the love of another, which is capable of healing any wound. All that is required is that you show up without agenda or reservation and move together to the healing dance of love.

Perhaps one partner continually wishes to lead while the other follows. Is there an unintegrated part of the feminine essence unable to find a home? Perhaps it would be wise to discuss together, or with a conscious counselor, the advantages of masculine/feminine integration and balance both in a body and within the relationship. The most successful spiritual partnerships occur when the masculine and feminine essences ebb and flow together in perfect attunement to the rhythm of life.

And what if one partner frequently leaves the dance floor, leaving the other to dance alone? This dance of beloveds requires that all show up, unquestioningly in the life of the other as the divine gifts that they are. Fear, trepidation, and disillusionment are meant to challenge the relationship and to test the seaworthiness of the craft they are sailing together. Without the safety net of trust that binds one to the other, knowing that whatever challenges may arise they are committed to facing them together, there will not be the incentive to forge ahead in tandem. Leave no doubt with your partner that you see them in the radiance of their soul being and are committed to address life's challenges together, no matter what. The strength of this promise and the demonstration of its applications in all aspects of life bind you to an unsinkable ship of light that no one can capsize.

Be it on the dance floor or in the surf of life, the seaworthiness of relationships is tested daily. The closer you hold each other, not in a death-grip, but in the freedom of an open palm, the more you will be able to weather the storms together. This is a demonstration of the trust you have, in and for each other, and binds you ever closer at the heart. Be willing to hold your beloved without tethers; just as two hearts in undulating harmony, touching at the conjuncture of hearts with the divine; dancing joyously in the hand of God… Mary Anna

Divine Partnership

As you move into a closer association with your beloved, there is something we would like to impress upon you. First, this is a holy association in that it is a commitment between the partners and God. Now your vision of that may be different, given the distortion of that concept by the various religious doctrines that have attempted to explain and control their vision of God. It is really a commitment to each other and to the prime Creator to respectfully engage in a relationship that honors the others in all ways. There can be nothing, shameful, dirty, or degrading therein because it honors the highest aspects of the divine partnership.

This is not to say that it is not to be uplifting and joyful in the extreme. Imagine having a beloved and God in your corner, creating experiences that hear, embrace, uplift and affirm your every move without recrimination, jealousy, admonition or doubt! Would that not free you from earthly concerns and allow you to float free on a magic carpet of loving energy and create great joy? We thought so.

Be willing to discard all else to the contrary. For their own reasons, "friends" and relatives may all have their opinions about the relationship, based upon their own less-than-honoring experiences. These are irrelevant and part of their own path to learning. You and your beloved are creating a new paradigm of loving interaction that is circumventing these old ego traps. You may wish to explain to them why this is different, given your commitment to God and each other or merely lead by example. The main thing is not to buy into the negativity because that is not the path you two have chosen.

Also, be aware that there are potholes on the path, lovingly placed there for your growth and healing. Be willing to come together with your beloved and lovingly examine each of them in partnership with God to see the lessons it is showing you. This is an opportunity to repair this and heal the blemish once and for all so that it will not need to recur. How joyous that you have a partner who understands and is committed to the process rather than picking at the unhealed wound. You are truly divine gifts to each other.

And finally, we might add... it behooves both to come together often in prayerful appreciation of all you are to each other and to the One. By "getting" these lessons and releasing them, you help increase the vibration of the planet and hasten the awakening of the masses. Be in gratitude for each other and the opportunity to be of service to the divine plan for humanity that you have chosen through your commitment to Hieros Gamos. This is the loving contract with God that will transform humanity into the One. Namaste,

Mary Anna

Conflict Resolution

As I have shared, the arena of conscious relationships offers many opportunities for growth and understanding. It is through the eyes of our intimate partners that we get the clearest glimpse of ourselves as divine beings as well as where we may be lacking and need additional refinement. This is not always welcomed because it calls us to relinquish our illusions of the ego and to see ourselves as flawed images of the divine to which we aspire. It is, however, the greatest opportunity for growth and understanding when one is able to see this disparity and the loving intention behind the mirror in order to adjust one's actions in the world.

Now frequently this image is too incongruent for us to process. It brings up things that we are not ready to address for they are in contrast to the idealized image we wish to display to our beloved. This is when things get tricky and one or both may slip back into a pattern of anger, blame and retribution. Neither wants to be seen as anything but perfection in the eyes of the beloved when one is still in shame and denial of their shortcomings. Until there is a surrender to the other in love, there will continue to be a barrier to growth and understanding.

Once both have surrendered to the magic of Hieros Gamos, the marriage of divine aspects of the masculine and feminine, the real journey begins. It is as if in the physical merging, this has created a new entity of wholeness embodying both individuals into the One. Any sore spots for one become an ache for the other until they are healed together. It requires complete honesty and transparency as both bring their "A game" to the higher entity that is coalescing. The little needs of the individuals are weighed against the collective needs of the partnership in seeking a loving resolution. Where there is a significant impact on the relationship by one choice over the other, there must be a commitment to work together until both are comfortable with the agreement.

Now this is not to say that individual opportunities for growth should be sacrificed if conflicts are more about process than a difference in values. It behooves discussion until both partners are comfortable with a decision to either allow one approach to be the approach for the partnership or a third alternative agreed upon that honors aspects of each view. If there is not conscious agreement between the partners, this will become a festering sore that will erupt in moments of stress and anger.

Where wounds are deeper and aggravate unhealed wounds that are waiting to be healed, it is better to acknowledge this as something to be addressed together. Conversations that do not blame or condemn are on a healing path that lead to discovery and revelation.

If each party only expresses how something is affecting them without projecting or blaming the other, it gives a clearer mirror to the other for examination, without feeling they must defend or explain their actions. Owning your emotions and reactions and not blaming them upon actions or inactions of the other is a significant pattern of growth and understanding that will help you transcend the challenges in your life and in your relationships.

There is a great opportunity for growth of the partnership when each is able to move in the world in positive ways and bring the experience back to share with the other. This works best when the partners are able to alternate these experiences, leapfrog fashion, rather than it being totally one-sided. It is a dynamic pattern of growth and mutual understanding that helps keep relationships fluid and dynamic.

The conflicts one experiences in the theatre of relationships is an important tool to help you move swiftly through the process of self-realization. The more you are able to step out of the ego viewpoint and allow the beloved to describe lovingly and compassionately how this is showing up for them, the more you will be able to use this dramatic process of transformation to catapult each other onto a higher spiritual path, hand in hand. Hold each other tightly and you will glide easily over the bumps on the path.

Much love,
Mary Anna

Divine Healing

As you come into resonance with each other you will notice that the things about the beloved that used to endear you may no longer be as alluring. Likewise, the things that used to irritate you are showing up more clearly as mirrors of things within yourself to be addressed together. Such is the journey of the beloveds. Intimate relationships are the greatest opportunity for growth in tandem and allow the magnification of intimacy to heal our wounds and blemishes in loving ways.

As for how you might go about accomplishing this, we might first wish to clarify that there is nothing "wrong" with either. Each is a product of their journey in this life and the evolution of the soul through countless incarnations. You have come together because each of you has unique gifts to share with the other and have a commitment at the soul level to help heal the woundings with love. There is nothing shameful or wrong with either. It is a wonderful opportunity to be a conduit and receiver of God's love and grace in the nurturing arms of the beloved.

Healing comes when all fear, anxiety, and shame are released. When one no longer feels the burden of past, painful lessons and has made the energetic shift into a new reality, the need for the experience of that lesson is released and healing begins. This can be instantaneous or a prolonged process depending on how long we hold on to it or "pick at the wound" with fear and doubt. All healing is a choice at the soul level to acknowledge, accept responsibility, release and give thanks for the lesson in order to move on. The sooner you are able to move through this process; the quicker healing will take place. The role of the beloveds is to hold this mirror for each other in order to make this possible.

As to how this can occur in the intimacy of a relationship, we might suggest that coming together frequently, and regularly, to hold each other in the light in meaningful conversation should be a top priority. Without the healing balm of the other's presence and attention, it is easy to let minor injuries fester and become serious in nature. Intimate sharing with each other not only the events in their lives but how these are bringing up feelings and emotions allows them to be processed at a conscious level and released.

Being able to view a situation from both a masculine and feminine viewpoint is an extremely helpful tool of understanding. By truthfully and honestly taking an observer stance of the situations in our lives and how we are reacting to them we can usually trace them to the underlying situation that precipitated the lesson in the first place so that healing can begin. Frequently we react, not to the situation at hand, but because it unearths deeply buried wounds that have never been able to heal properly. Your beloved is there to help you through this process by lovingly holding this mirror of awareness, without judgment or admonishment.

This is the beauty of the gift of Hieros Gamos, fully expressed in loving awareness and commitment to each other and the journey together. Embrace each other in this loving energy and all is healed in love.

Much Love, Mary Anna

Divine Comedy

Part of your divine journey together is to help each other fully express your divine qualities. What does this really mean, you might well ask? For starters, we might suggest that you begin by seeing the face of God reflected in your partner's eyes. While all of his/her actions may not yet express that holy image right now, this is a work-in-progress gifted to you to reflect your own divine qualities as well. Each of you must be committed to help the other grow into this divine image.

The trick in doing this is that it is also a lesson on how to accomplish it and learn together in love. Past tactics may have been that in order to correct negative behavior, you may have begun by pointing out where they fell short of your expectations and they could either shape up or the game was over. How different might be the outcome and with far fewer resentments if instead of pointing out where they miss the mark and shaming them into compliance, you were to joyfully commend the things they did accomplish of a positive nature, and how much it means to you that they are working on the rest. By offering your support and assistance in the process it becomes a shared endeavor and encouragement to reach higher and shine brighter in your beloved's eyes.

This is just a small example of how beloveds are learning to work together to enhance their relationships and draw them in closer alignment with their God-self. Divine partnerships are based upon the triangular model. If all decisions are made under the auspicious presence of divine countenance, it elevates the participants to step into their divine presence as well. The holy trinity is both masculine and feminine working in concert with God.

Is there a holy part of the relationship but also one that continues to operate in a third-dimensional environment? Of course, but this is where you begin to try on the clothes of a higher vibration and "break them in" and practice until it becomes second nature. If instead of allowing yourselves to be drawn back into old patterns of blame and defense, how different might it be to catch yourself before and ask your partner for an uninterrupted conference call with your divine selves. By clearly expressing what is going on within you to your beloved and consciously listening to how this is being heard and processed by them, you are able to set the stage for meaningful dialogue without escalating into an argument of fear, blaming, resentment, and anger.

Be able to stand back and allow your divine selves to look at the disruption, the triggers, the reactions, and the patterns that are playing out. What deeper lessons are you processing together? How is it helping you to recognize the deeper wounds and allow them to surface for airing and healing? How is your beloved unknowingly, or not, playing into this sacred dance together?

This is the "work" of relationships that clears the area so that play can take place. The more you become comfortable with the process, the quicker it will become to resolve and to see the humor in this dance together. There is great irony and mirth to be found in the pathetic dance humans sometimes engage in as they skirt around the core issues wanting to be addressed in their lives.

The sooner you are able to see your own choreography and how you use the activity in your life to avoid and hide the core issues your soul is trying to reveal to you, the more amusement you will have in being able to poke fun at this ridiculous attempt to mask your divine nature. The truth that is waiting to be revealed is waiting for your beloved's gentle touch. In this tender embrace, all things are possible and divinely orchestrated. Allow this dance to play out together and you will soon see the beauty and the absurdity underlying the process. God is smiling too...

Mary Anna

The Three-Legged Stool

As you begin to come together as a couple, we have a few suggestions as to how you might wish to proceed. First, be sure that you retain your sovereignty as individuals in the process. This is a triangular association with the two partners and the third being the relationship. Like a three-legged stool, it requires the integrity of all of the legs to function. Do not feel that by "sacrificing" yourself and all you bring to the relationship you will enhance the process. It takes two whole, healthy, well-balanced partners to create the strength of the relationship.

Second we might suggest that you think in terms of doing all you can to be the embodiment of health, vitality, and integrity. Do not expect the other to make up for any slacking on your part in these areas. The success of this partnership requires that all bring their "A game" to the process. It is time to clean up your act and become what you desire in the other.

Third we might suggest that you become familiar with the concept of unconditional love. This is not, as some believe, being willing to forgive the other's faults. It is belief that in the merging of the two into One there is an all-encompassing caring, respect, kindness, and compassion for the other that mirrors what you feel for yourself. There are no conditions or requirements by which this love would be withheld. They are an extension of your being.

Now this is not to say that there will not be things within the relationship that will annoy or disappoint you, but that these are things that you will work on honestly and consciously to resolve so that both of you are on the same page. Our soul contract with our beloved is to be mirrors of these differences, but it is also an opportunity and commitment to see that they are resolved and healed together. You might wish to see your beloved as an extension of your soul sent in grace to help elevate you to a higher vibrational platform. He/she is there to do that for you as well. This is indeed a group process of enlightenment.

As you move together in tandem of souls, you will begin to build the third part of this process which is the relationship. As with anything, the quality of the relationship will depend on the attention, devotion, and commitment the parties put forth in creating and maintaining it. If it is something that is sandwiched between other activities in the day, that sliver will be what it looks like. If, however you both carve out special, uninterrupted time for each other to explore the intricacies of your dance together and how you can grow and fan the flame of love, you will create an equally healthy third leg on this stool of partnership.

No loving partnership is without challenges; it is what allows it to strengthen and grow. The test will be to see if the partners can release their desire to address these separately or if they are willing to come together and find a common solution. This requires a great deal of trust in each other which will continue to build, the more they work together to find a common solution.

It is not the job of either to "fix" the other, but to work together to find an avenue of experience that honors the unique gifts each brings to the altar of relationship. You are your brother/sister's keeper because you hold their heart in tenderness and allow it to grow into the magnificence of the process of Hieros Gamos. We wish you all of this and more.

Mary Anna

Juicing the Ride

The connection between you and your beloved is enhanced to the extent that you are able to meet each other in the higher realm of conscious, sacred partnership. When each individual essence agrees to merge into One, there becomes a fertile field for growth and understanding. As for how this might play out in the world of form, we have a few suggestions:

First, as you allow all of the "shoulds", needs and wants of the ego to shift into the background, you are able to see more clearly, not only the soul of the other but how you might assist this extension of yourself in scaling the walls of self-realization. If our focus is less about self, and more about assisting another in growth and understanding, our own journey is enhanced and magnified ten-fold in the process.

If each decision is made in concert with the other with the overriding theme being whether it is supportive of building a sacred partnership, there will be little veering off the path to this exalted goal. When in question, the ultimate arbitrator should be how this might serve God and the relationship. This is an opportunity to clearly define the path to enlightenment when both parties hold the light for each other and choose a common route out of the darkness.

Third, we might suggest, joy is the juice that powers sacred relationships. If you can find the path of joy together, you will be more inclined to stay committed. What gives you joy and how can you convey this every day to your partner? If you rose each day with the singular purpose of bringing joy to the life of your beloved, how would you enhance your journey together? How many relationships fall into disrepair because they have failed to keep the fires that brought them together fed and nourished? Find a way each day to bring joy into the life of your beloved.

Do not allow a day to pass without expressing the things within your heart that endear them to you. Sometimes it is the nonverbal gestures that speak the loudest. A smile, a knowing glance alluding to shared secrets, a thoughtful gift from the heart, a devotion to something they care about, all demonstrate to the other that they are loved, appreciated and cherished beyond measure.

Loving partnerships require continuing reinforcement to withstand not only the temptations but the challenges of a world full of distractions. Being able to honestly discuss with the other challenges to staying on the path of fidelity is a sign of maturity in the relationship and trust. This requires that both partners not only are secure in their own commitment but are willing to put the doubts and challenges on the altar of the relationship to work with God to resolve any momentary misjudgments that might disturb the equilibrium.

The challenges that are faced consciously and with love and forgiveness will become the bedrock and foundation for the growing process of Hieros Gamos that will only come when there is absolute trust in the fidelity of the other. Baring your soul in truth and honesty and trusting that they will honor and heal any imperfections unlocks the door to higher achievement. Be willing to step out of your third-dimensional egoic state with all of its misperceptions and judgments and enter the sanctity of sacred partnership and you will experience the joy inherent in the process.

We wish you great joy… Mary Anna

Divine Communication

If it feels like you are surfing the cusp between dimensions, perhaps this is actually the case. As you begin to take on the qualities of your divine self, you begin to realize how little of the "real" world is operating in this frequency. The more you trod the higher path, the more the traffic clears out and the less interference you experience with those around you. As you begin to see more clearly your own role in the patterns of life, you will find that you attract to you those who are there to assist you in the work you are doing together. This goes for the partners in relationship that are ready to take this next step.

So how do you go about discerning whether you are ready to experience the higher aspects of a loving relationship? First we might suggest that it requires that both partners be on the same spiritual track. One cannot force awareness in the other. Certainly, one can and should express their truth and understanding, but it cannot be forced upon the other or made a prerequisite that there be total agreement on all things.

The process of growth requires that we be willing to listen and thoughtfully go within to see how this registers on a personal level. One of the advantages of a soulful relationship is that each is free to bring in their own observations and assessments to share with their partner so that both may benefit from the experience. As long as there is no coercion to conform, but a willingness to learn from each other, this is a dynamic process of spiritual growth and understanding that is not possible alone.

We might also suggest that both partners be encouraged to engage in the world around them in different and meaningful ways. The experience of being in an expanded environment of experience broadens the reach of their understanding and feeds the conversations that will be precipitated by their observations of how this is playing out in their lives. There is an added benefit of having more eyes with which to see the world that facilitates the process of growth together. Since the masculine and feminine do view the world differently, it is immensely helpful if each shares their unique perception of events and processes for feedback from their complement. This gives a more balanced view of the situation and allows each to see and experience aspects of the process that are not visible alone. This becomes something called leapfrogging where each party is able to move freely in the world, blazing the way for the other to move ahead. The more such experiences they are able to process together, the greater will be the level of trust and understanding that develops between them.

It is no accident that the fifth, or throat, chakra is the gateway to the divine. If we are to be as One, it is imperative that we are able to communicate with the other parts. This is not to say that this must be an intellectual download where we share all of the minutia of our lives without getting to the underlying meaning and purpose. We would like to suggest that it would be more beneficial to share the things we struggle with in order to get insights beyond our own ego perceptions. As we share our process with each other, the challenges, and the insights, we develop a deep understanding and appreciation of the things that brought us together and how we have the missing pieces in each other's puzzle.

Non-verbal communication is also important because it can convey many things we may be reluctant to express verbally. We all have felt the passive-aggressive expressions of disapproval such as eye-rolling or rigid body postures that express emotions not verbalized; but what of other more positive reassurances of our love and support? You show your caring and attentiveness as well as your love every time you pat, touch, caress, and physically reach out to your beloved. This is not necessarily PDA for all to see, but unspoken reassurance that you are there, you care, and you are with them in the moment and beyond.

Communication is one of the most important pieces of your journey together. It can remove many of the impediments to loving awareness. If you know, without a doubt, of the intentions, feelings, and actions of your partner because you have discussed it and shared the yearnings and the longings of your heart, you are able to withstand any onslaughts the world may bring to your door together. Betrayals occur when things are unsaid and the underlying needs, struggles, and motivations are not discussed and dealt with in non-judgmental ways. An issue for one becomes an issue for both when it is processed on the altar of the relationship. Allow your beloved entrance to the musings of your soul and you will ever endear them and invite a like response.

Hieros Gamos is possible when both are able to share their deepest soul longings and find the fulfillment of these in their beloved's arms. Open your heart but also your mouth for this is the gateway to the divine.

Mary Anna

Sacred Partnership

The intention to have a conscious sacred partnership begins the process of manifestation of this reality. As long as both keep this vision clearly in their intention, all else will fall into place. If we allow the illusions of the ego to distract us from the prime purpose of the relationship, which is a deeper understanding of the experience of loving awareness, we will find it difficult to keep on this narrow path.

Part of your commitment to each other is to daily renewal of this promise, no matter what the circumstances of your life may be. It is easy to take things for granted when enmeshed in the minutia of life in a third-dimensional environment. However, this is all-the-more important that you make time for your first priority, which is your relationship. This need not be lengthy, or time consuming, but there should be reassurance to each other that they are ever in our thoughts and are held in a sacred place in the heart.

As we hold the light for each other there will be times when one shines brighter than the other. This is part of the dance of the beloveds as they ebb and flow together in perfect harmony. It allows us to provide the assistance the other requires in times of stress and discouragement and to receive gratefully when the situations are reversed.

As to the receiving part...those who have mastered the lesson of giving from our abundance sometimes have difficulty in being on the receiving end. Part of your dance together is to learn to be grateful receivers of the abundant love of God, held in the arms of the beloved. Until we are able to gratefully receive the divine gift, there will not be a balance of energetic flow and the process will be thwarted.

Realizing your own worthiness to receive all of the gifts of divine partnership is a major factor in opening the floodgates of divine blessings. When you accept and embrace the fact that you are made in God's image, and by honoring yourself, you also honor your inherent divinity, thus facilitating the process of manifestation of divine love in all aspects of your life. If you are held in the hand of God, how could you expect less?

Once you are able to move past this impediment to understanding, a world of possibilities opens for your enjoyment. In divine partnership with a beloved who is an extension of yourself and you of them, is there anything beyond your reach? We thought so. So, what might you wish to create with this divine clay? What are the longings of your soul that have been calling to you for fulfillment but have been put on the back burner? As you come into resonance with your awakened self, what is no longer beyond the realm of possibilities and longing for completion? If things seemed impossible as a limited being, what has changed now that you are empowered by your divine complement?

Spend time together reimagining the possibilities of a world without barriers to the things that call to your soul for fulfillment. This is a divine gift for each other that can open up an expanded world of possibilities if you are willing to set aside the old barriers to creation. Step together through the veil of possibilities and we assure you, there is a new world in the making awaiting your participation. Hand in hand, in loving awareness, all things are possible... Mary Anna

Divine Creation

The journey together into consciousness requires a level of openness that has not been experienced in the "real" world. While belief systems have their tenants that one must adhere to in order to be considered one of the flock, the journey together in divine partnership requires none. This is a blank slate longing to be filled together. So, what do you wish to create within the realm of your sacred union? We might suggest that you begin by coming together in expression of your dreams, desires and inspirations. In the expression of these inner visions there will be revealed the overlapping path that you are being invited to trod together. You each have pieces of each other's puzzle waiting to be brought forth.

This missing puzzle piece is frequently an idea or ability that called to you in your youth but was buried in the minutia of life. You came in with intentions to create a higher vision of reality in some way but have not had the inspiration until now to make it so. This is your opportunity to dust off the secret longings of your soul and see the world of possibilities with new eyes.

Soul driven inspirations frequently seem somewhat fanciful given third-dimensional consciousness but that is what makes them so inspired. You finally have someone who can dream the impossible with you and point out the possibilities you may have missed. What might be the missing piece you may have overlooked that moves this into the realm of the attainable?

As you look at the hopes and dreams of your beloved, how might you assist in their creation? How does it free you from the drudgery of the finite to journey together into realms of the unachieved? Unlimited possibilities are there for you when you join in the adventure of many lifetimes. Once you have removed the impediments to creation, all things become reality.

So, what might be preventing this from happening? We might suggest that past experience again looms in the forefront, perpetuating the status quo. If no one were willing to try something, or if others have failed, there is every reason to believe that it might be impossible to achieve. However, this is an opportunity to see things with new eyes. Together you have keys to discovery that were not there before. As you work together in the bond of partnership, there will be new insights that reveal hidden passageways or illuminate pitfalls that went unnoticed before. Allow yourselves to soar over barriers of past failures because together you open a whole new realm of opportunities for exploration.

There is a new world in process, fueled by the dynamic energy of divine partnerships. At each other's side, worlds are being created with the balance of feminine/masculine energy that has been missing from prior attempts. It is in this balance of equals that many will move hand in hand into the new paradigm of divine creation. This is the promise of Hieros Gamos.

Mary Anna

Archetypes of Wholeness

As you come into emotional resonance with your beloved, it is important to be aware of the different pieces you hold for the other and the ones you withhold for yourself. While the completed entity of the relationship holds the aspects of both the masculine and feminine in balance, it is important for each to be comfortable in their respective sexual essence and the polarity of those. Now this is not to say that relationships of the same gender cannot experience sacred partnerships, but only that, in order for balance to be attained, the sexual essence of the partners must be in complement.

For wholeness to be achieved, it is important for all of the archetypes to be represented in a sacred relationship. For this to happen, each may choose to embody different aspects of the divine in complement to the other. For instance, one may hold the protector piece and the other the priestess or sage until their partner is able to step in that aspect of him/herself. Where there is conflict, it is usually where both are vying for the same piece in competition. The dance of beloveds is that they model the process for each other until they are able to step into that template themselves.

There are no requirements that any aspect be either masculine or feminine. We all go through many steps on our journey into wholeness. Different partners over a lifetime help you perfect different aspects of your completeness as you embody more and more of your divine qualities. Different people in your life may hold different mirrors for you and you for them. This is a graphic example of how the pieces fit together in the divine matrix. If you embrace the highest demonstration of each of the soul qualities in the archetypes, you will eventually bring all together into the wholeness your soul desires.

Hieros Gamos, Genter

We invite you to join with your beloved on a journey into the heart where all aspects of your divine self are represented in their fullest expression of loving energy. This is the dance of the beloveds. Mary Anna

Penny's Thoughts

Healthy, fulfilling relationships are more likely to be found in those who have experienced life, learned lessons, and embody more aspects of their archetypical patterning. They have learned to work in concert with their partners who possess their missing or complementary parts in mutually agreed upon, supportive ways. Partnerships that honor and support each other's growth, gifts, and abilities allow for others, who may have complementary pieces as well, to join in and are expanding the definition and experience of working together in the Oneness of the new paradigm.

We are complex people with many abilities and interests. How boring and limiting it would be to have a soulmate who mirrored your every mood and desire perfectly. We come together as divine complements to learn and grow together and to support each other in filling out our dance cards of experience. This may take more than one person to have the full range of desires and abilities that complement your own. This is where soul groups come in. In your circle of friends and acquaintances there are others who have missing pieces of your life plan. Life therefore becomes a scavenger hunt to find and utilize all the parts of you that are being held in the safekeeping of others. Relationships are a vehicle for that to happen.

Relationships in the New Paradigm

You may have noticed how your relationships are morphing into a different frequency. As more and more soulmates find each other they are able to help each other remove the shackles of limited perception that have tethered them to the past ways of being together. You are finding that old conventions such as marriage are no longer the limiting forms they once were, based on scarcity and competition. In a society based upon love, there are many ways that we can love each other that are not bound by the tethers and restrictions of conventional marriage.

As your world becomes more complex, there will be more freedom to find the pieces of relationships that nourish your soul and perhaps join with others in community to complete your missing parts. While there will always be partnerships based upon procreation, that need not be the only purpose in coming together with complementary souls. There are many ways of forming intimate unions, and many of them do not include physical intimacy. How intimate a journey is it with another that shares one's deepest soul longings and experiences? How does this compare with physical couplings based merely upon physical attraction? You are redefining the pieces of your world and honoring the deeper intentions of your purpose together which may be quite different from the old paradigm of marriage.

You are entering into a new era of sacred partnerships where you can choose whether or not to enter into a physical intimacy. This in no way negates the power of the relationship, only that this is or is not part of the dynamic.

So how do you go about assessing the relationships in your life and what you contribute to the growth and understanding of each other? We might suggest that it is a process of wholeness. If both parties are whole and complete they are likely to be able to live together harmoniously but there may be few challenges that would be a catalyst to growth. If such is the case, perhaps the purpose of their journey together is to mirror and teach and hold the light for others on how to achieve balance and understanding in their journey together.

If prospective partners are experiencing voids in some area of their wholeness, they will naturally attract those who can irritate these raw edges and precipitate a healing response. This assumes that both are committed to the process of growth and understanding. Realize that this can also create a site of trauma if healing is not a common goal. It will take repeated woundings and healing to overcome the past hurts unless the balm of forgiveness is part of the process. This is an opportunity to cut through the old processing and go directly to the grace of forgiveness to circumvent the traumas of the past.

Love cannot be bound and when we try to restrict its movement we only stifle the flame longing to be expressed. If we are to truly love another, we must believe ourselves whole and capable of sustaining and nurturing that love or we will extinguish the flame. We are truly free of our illusions about love when we can hold it in open palms, knowing that it will be there as long as we do not crush it with our own illusions of self-doubt and unworthiness. We are free by freeing others to express their own reflection of our divine selves to each other, whatever that looks like and for however long it might last. I AM

Journey of the Chakras

It behooves you to look deeper into the meaning and purpose of your romantic associations. All are drawn together in physical attraction but there is also a deeper soul-purpose playing out. When you look deep into each other's eyes, do you see and feel a connection that transcends time and space? This is the window into the soul that you have come together to experience.

Now all of this may seem to be a process of the mind that is analyzing what should be an emotional experience of discovering love, but we would like to point out that it is a coming together of all aspects of our multidimensional being in balance that will activate all of the tumblers and unlock the sacred space where Hieros Gamos can take place.

You will undoubtedly feel an attraction that ignites the lower chakras. Do not discount this because this "early warning system" is a subtle energy recognition that there is a frequency match that is worth exploring. Is this partner interested, willing, and capable of opening the doors that root us to the seminal experiences of our journey? Are we open and willing to join them on the soul journey that will bring up many of the unhealed wounds of this, and previous, incarnations for healing? Is our attraction great enough to fuel this commitment to growth and healing? This is calling us to step into our soul journey together.

As you experience all of the joys, challenges, and disappointments of the physical aspects of union, you have the opportunity to use these powerful feelings to heal each other in the intimacy of the physical. The ecstasy of the experience plants seeds of remembrance of your divine nature and beckons you Home. Your partner becomes the vehicle for healing and growth, if you consciously make this a priority and are not frightened away by fear and insecurity. This is the healer your soul has sent to draw you back into your remembrance of your divine nature if you are willing to move beyond your level of comfort and touch the face of God.

You will have to develop a level of trust and acceptance to move past the gates of the third chakra into the regions of the heart. This is where all of your wounding that has taken place in the lower chakras gets processed. Until this is recognized and healed, there is very little possibility of moving into the upper chakras for illumination. Time spent with the beloved revealing, exploring, and loving the difficult lessons of our growth will develop the muscles of trust that will support the journey into a loving relationship.

As for love, this is the mature plant that grows from the soil of the first chakra, is fertilized and watered in the second and strengthened and protected in the third. The process of growth requires that you move through these stages in order to reach full maturity in the level of the heart. The experience of love is a journey into the heart that awakens the emotions and allows them to grow. While this is not the totality of the expression of mature love, fully realized, it is the necessary training ground for higher possibilities. The journey to Hieros Gamos requires the development and mastery of the four lower chakras in order to express the full flowering as we move into the realm of the divine.

One of the primary skills of divine mastery is being able to fearlessly and honestly articulate your truth. There must be mastery to the extent that you understand, accept, appreciate, and are willing to share the efforts of your journey that have brought you to the place of personal mastery. As you move into the higher levels, the journey into Oneness means that vestiges of the little self, or ego, slip into the background as you move into the Oneness of your divine nature. This is where you are inviting your beloved to join you in creating the third entity of relationship. This requires that both be evenly matched and committed to the process and to holding each other in this light. This requires exercising their gifts and abilities to articulate to each other their inner thoughts, feelings, and emotions so that they can move together into the higher realms.

The journey into the sixth chakra together is one of wonder and revelation. As you move past the barriers of the physical world you begin to connect with each other telepathically. You instinctively know what the other is processing and are able to supply missing pieces for their use. It is as if you have merged at an intuitive level and have coordinated your efforts and responses into a dance of complementary parts operating in the world but not of it. You know at a deeper level what your beloved's response will be to a situation and are able to flow effortlessly together in a divine dance. All challenges are met calmly and consciously with each supplying missing pieces to the other's process.

As you move together into the higher realm, you are able to see the face of God mirrored in the beloved. You each hold pieces of the divinity of the other that are merged in the atmosphere that permeates all of your interactions.

*This is not just in a dreamy state of Samadhi (*a state of intense concentration achieved through meditation. In Hindu yoga, this is regarded as the final state at which union with the divine is achieved) *but is reflected in all of the third-dimensional activities you participate in together. You reflect the presence of God, fully embodied in a divine partnership that is obvious to all you meet. You are emissaries of divine presence modeled in form to help guide others Home to their own divinity. You are love personified as One...*

Mary Anna

At the Door of the Temple

"Tell me friends – is there one among you who would not awake from the slumber of life if love touched your soul with its fingertips?

Who among you would not sail the distant seas, cross the deserts and climb the topmost peaks to meet the woman who his soul has chosen?

What youth's heart would not follow to the ends of the world the maiden with the aromatic breath, sweet voice and magic soft hands that had enraptured his soul?

What being would not burn his heart as incense, before God who listens to supplications grants his prayers?"

Kahlil Gabran

Experiencing Hieros Gamos

As one of the exercises in a lesson on attracting our energetic partner we talked about listing all of the things we were looking for in a romantic partner. I began by thinking of how I wished to feel in a relationship and the characteristics a partner might have that could help bring that about. I purposefully listed no specifics as to age, wealth, physical endowments, or circumstances so that the universe could fill in the blanks in ways greater than I could imagine. The things most important to me are character traits and values that would define how we come together in complementary resonance.

I thought of the friends that know me best and have my best interest at thought. Who would be better at introducing me to someone they know who they believe would best be a good partner for me? I gave them the list and asked for them to be on the lookout for my partner so that they could introduce me.

Jerry

In the meantime, I got the feeling that it was time to go back on the internet and explore the larger dating market then in our small town. I had done that before and while it did not yield the romantic partner I was looking for; I did meet many soul brothers that have had a positive effect on my life. I was guided to a particular site and put together my profile, including my list of what I was looking for. I was in the process of posting my pictures when I received an e-mail from the only candidate that caught my attention. He said that he was strongly attracted to the energy in my profile, even though he had not seen my picture yet and wanted to find out more about me. I responded favorably and gave him my home e-mail address. His immediate response let me know that this man was not tentative and definitely sensed something in me that others had not seen. After a couple of e-mail exchanges and a subsequent phone call we decided that this was definitely something worth exploring. I dowsed and he was everything on my list!

Jerry lived three hours away but wanted to drive to where I live and go with me to church where I am a Chaplain. He used to live here and attend the same church but left just before I arrived in Sedona. He has spent the previous two years healing and clearing of wounds and fears and was whole, healed, and healthy and ready to begin a new relationship without fetters. We agreed to meet prior to the service at McDonalds for coffee and go together to church.

So how do we go about recognize those who we have a soul commitment with?

In *Destiny of Souls*, Michael Newton, Ph.D. talks about how we sometimes agree on a sign before incarnating so we will recognize each other. Many times, we see the connection in each other's eyes. When we first gazed into each other's eyes, there was a deep knowing that this was not an ordinary experience. He says my eyes lit up with sparks, unlike anything he had ever seen before.

When I walked in, he embraced me and we both felt the magnetic attraction brought forward from many lifetimes together that staggered us in its intensity and has not diminished. The more the synchronicities began revealing themselves, it became immediately obvious that this was a divine assignment with God's fingerprint all over it.

We both have reached an age where we have experienced love in its imitation forms, and this was not even in the same universe with those baby steps. There is a deep knowing on both sides that this is not an ordinary experience of "chemistry" though that is certainly part of the process. Beyond all "logic" we both knew that this was the beloved who was there to experience all of the aspects of Hieros Gamos together – again and again.

As is my process, I asked Mother Mary Anna what we were together to experience. This was her reply:

My dearest Penny,

As we told you before, this is a man of much potential in your life. While it may seem you have just begun your journey together, in fact this is something that spans many lifetimes. You have long ago resolved the impediments to love that you came with and now this is time to experience the full expression of this most sacred emotion, fully expressed in your body and your lives. We said that this would be something that you would be sharing with others and now you are able to experience what that looks, feels, tastes like in its most exquisite form. It is the full amplification of the principles of Christly love.

We do not mean that one should worship the other, but rather that if you begin to see the perfection of the inner being of the other as fully formed expression of your divine compliment, you will move closer to this exalted ideal. Beneath the tarnish and dents inflicted by a world that is not yet resonating with divine energy is the soul of your beloved, waiting for your tender kiss to bring it alive once more. This is the fulfillment of not just the fairy tale of romance, but fully realized divinity when both step up to this sacred process.

Your life together will take on a magical quality. Both of you have transcended many lessons on the earth school that, though sometimes painful, have brought you to this place today where you are finally able to scale this higher peak together, hand in hand. The challenges of before are history as you are moving in a state of grace and wonder. Both of you feel the difference in the density of the world around you and how this is somehow transcended in your embrace. When you come together physically in the profound and loving way that you have, you finally begin to see what we mean about uniting the upper chakras with the heart. This is the narrow path to divinity but first you must cross the chasm of fears, doubts, and separation to experience love in this exalted state.

As to what you will do with this divine knowledge, we have a few suggestions. After you experience the joy of your journey together and have fully grounded this in your being, you may wish to share the premise and the process with others. You are the poster couple for the meaning of Hieros Gamos as expressed in form. Allow your hearts to open wide enough to invite in others with ears to hear. It is time and you are divine love personified. To enter the arms of the beloved as a little child and be held in the ecstasy of the beloved in the hand of God is a journey few appreciate the significance of. We thank you for your participation in this divine adventure of fully realized love and know that you will not be disappointed as we move forward together in the light.

Be love, Mary Anna

Both of us are moral, responsible, highly functioning adults. The mere suggestion that we would do anything as "irresponsible" as sharing a life with someone who we just met and knew little about was unthinkable in conventional thinking but made perfect sense to us and those we know who know us and are tuned into a different reality in Sedona. When it is right and we listen to our heart as well as our genitals we KNOW and without fear, are able to move with the magic.

When we hugged on our first meeting there was such a powerful feeling of connection and inner knowing that this was to be a significant relationship that it was staggering for both of us. Within a few minutes, we both felt that we had known each other all our lives and still cannot believe that we have not been married for 20 years or more. We evidently brought in powerful soul memories from what I believe were two marriages in previous lifetimes and other significant relationships we have shared before.

While I am a dowser and used to calibrating the frequency of truth, this was confirmation for me that this was real. He, surprisingly, was just as certain about the relationship as I was. All of the things about me that other lesser men had discredited and feared, he embraced and valued. His quiet, unassuming presence obscured the depth, passion, and compassion that shallower women missed but I valued immensely. We began a soulful relationship that continues to astound us in its richness of the loving experience, beyond anything either of us has known before.

From the first kiss we shared on the eve of our first meeting, there was, as Mary Anna had predicted, *"a rekindling of fires left smoldering in previous lifetimes"*. In that kiss, the paradigm shifted. There was a beautiful, passionate exchange of sexual energy that is so honoring and powerful that it is beyond the realm of either of our earthly experience. As we moved through the processes shared by Mother Mary Anna, barriers to love in its highest form of expression dissolve and the feelings of total immersion in a field of loving energy are powerful and transforming.

As Mother Mary Anna told me *"It will be about compassion and honoring; about appreciation and caring on a level seldom known in your world. It will be about coming together in a full aspect of the One with reflection of the divine qualities of the masculine and feminine amplified in a higher appreciation of the divine in each other."* What she failed to mention was the totally "mind-blowing" experience sharing sexual love becomes when you offer your bodies as sacraments of love to your divine partner on the altar of sacred relationship.

It has been ten years since either of us were married or in a serious relationship. We are mature and aware enough that this romantic stage of any relationship will probably not last and we can eventually move into the power struggle stage. We consciously address this as we move together with what seems like seamless interaction. The thing that seems most important in maintaining this rarefied state is that neither of us have big ego issues that need massaging. We find that when we are focused upon making it a joyful experience for each other, it is for us as well. The more I give of myself without expectation because I know that it is something my beloved will appreciate, the more I receive in return without asking. And we do deeply appreciate not only this divine opportunity to experience love at this deep level but how this is elevating all of our experiences to these higher frequencies. Our cup runneth over with love. Would it will always be so…

This is not to say that it is without challenges for we are in the learning the stages of our dance and it is in stepping on each other's toes that we learn the rhythm and flow of our life together, forever altered by the love of our beloved. I find that these missteps are frequently precipitated when we deny ourselves in order to please the other and thus perpetrate a falsehood that will come back to challenge us. The more authentic we are with our beloved, the more we are to find a common path of truth and respect.

The Third Possibility

The first situation to be addressed was how we might combine our lives consciously without giving up the things that make us who we are. I have a house in Sedona that I share with housemates. I am a chaplain and very active in Unity of Sedona where I teach classes, volunteer, and counsel. There are many cultural, artistic and spiritual things there that call to us both. I have many friends and entertain frequently. He has lived for the past two years in an RV park in a small town in the desert 3 hours away where he was able to cocoon and heal emotionally and clear in the nurturing arms of nature. He has many friends that helped him through the process. It is a very masculine environment and Sedona is very feminine.

We have slept in each other's arms every night since we met and do not wish to be apart. At the same time, we wish to allow each other to continue to grow in the environment in which we thrive. He adores Sedona and is nourished by hiking the trails nearby my home, but he is also drawn to the desert. He has come to love and appreciate the "family" I have created in my home and enjoys interacting in that conscious, supportive, and exciting community. We discussed selling the RV and moving everything to Sedona. He began getting rid of the ATV, motorcycle and other toys. Luckily we rethought that process since it became more and more evident that there was a big difference in the quiet, contemplative, life he had led with nature in the Arizona desert and the active, involved one I have led in Sedona. While he was willing to give up his former life to join mine, I knew that he might come to resent that in time if he was not through with the experience.

When there are two conflicting possibilities, Mary Anna teaches, try to find a third solution that honors the needs of both. Together we went to the desert and began looking at the situation there with new eyes. As we removed all of the clutter of his bachelor life, the possibilities of a romantic getaway and retreat began to reveal themselves. The relaxed, simple atmosphere in the modest RV began to call to me as I had spent 1-1/2 years in one when we built a house during my previous marriage. I remembered the intimacy of working and playing together in close quarters and how beautiful that can be when there is deep love shared.

As we stripped the small bedroom of the twin bed and desk, there emerged a sacred space in which we celebrate our love. We vowed to leave everything but our love at the doorway and to devote our full attention to the cultivation of that blossoming presence. We brought in candles, scented oils, beautiful linens, soft pillows, beautiful music and a new bed in which to consummate our love. No computers, cell phones, TVs or distractions from the prime purpose of the space which is to nurture the relationship. It is magical and we feel the specialness of the life we are creating. According to him, he traded his "man cave" for a "boutique" but couldn't be happier because he now feels nurtured and loved.

During the day he is nourished by his meditative hikes in the desert where he feels so drawn and alive. I can read, write, meditate and even work on-line until we come back together to share our day. We both have wonderful friends in both places so by moving back and forth as we are able, it allows us to participate in the best of both worlds and grow our relationship by honoring both of our needs. Life is good.

The Intimate Dance

Neither Jerry nor I have ever experienced anything comparable to the intimate dance we are doing together. From the first time we embraced and experienced the magnetic energy that had drawn us to each other, there was no question that we had crossed a threshold into another dimension of experience. It felt so magical and compelling that we were almost afraid to speak of it less we break the spell. Wondrously, the more we shared the ecstatic feelings we were experiencing, the more real they became because the other was experiencing the same thing! We instantly began to experience feelings that seemed learned from another lifetime when we had been lovers of some magnitude. The familiarity of each other's bodies and movements were all stored in our cellular memory, waiting to be released.

Neither of us are what you might call promiscuous. I had three lovers in the ten years since Gordon had died. He had been celibate since his divorce ten years earlier. This was beyond our experience but both of us were feeling something that was not of this earthly reality. We tried to watch a movie together but the moment we kissed, the paradigm had shifted and there was no turning back. We both KNEW, unquestioningly that this was the real thing. I invited him into my room where it began to take form. All of the stirrings of youth were there but now we had the wisdom and dexterity of maturity to guide them through higher portals and avoid the known potholes of experience.

It is said that Solomon and Sheba stayed in the bridal chamber for a full cycle of the moon and we did that and more. We slept and loved in each other's arms every night (and day) since that first kiss. We are beloveds, and of that we have no doubt.

The beauty and the profundity of our lovemaking takes our breath away. The consequences of age have become gifts in that they have allowed us to experience love in more expanded ways that slow the process into an erotic dance of love that ebbs and flows in delicious spontaneity and takes us higher and deeper than we ever thought possible. The profound connection we both feel is amplified exponentially as we gaze deeply into each other's soul while we perform the sacraments of physical love that pleasures the other and connects us intimately with their body. There is no sense of separateness or manipulation. We are One. We gift each other freely and completely, without thought of compensation for the sheer pleasure of seeing the joy in our beloved's eyes and being part of participating in their pleasure.

I am not sure that without the preparation of the earlier lessons from Mother Mary Anna that we would have been ready for this quantum leap in lovemaking. I feel the presence of Mary Magdalene also as we are guided into physical expressions that unite the heart with the upper chakras. Verbally sharing our experiences, what gives us pleasure, things this might bring up for us, and just reaffirming the love we feel again and again, juices the ride. Removing all of the things that interfere with the full expression of our love including clothing, obstacles, inhibitions, and distractions allows the uninterrupted flow of energy between us. The more we step out of our awareness of time, space, and obligations and are open and present in the embrace of the other in the moment, the more we create that loving reality in the rest of our life. It is life lived in the frequency of love and we are indeed held in the hand of God and all is well. We are blessed and grateful.

Jerry is cute. People tell us we make a cute couple and I appreciate that. I never realized what a blessing that is in a relationship before. Cute is loveable but it is real. There is not a pretense that he is anything but that. Suave and debonair have their attraction but for a long distance, happy relationship I will take cute every time. There can be a playful, magical, pixie-like quality to cute that helps you giggle together over the absurdities of life and not take the challenges too seriously. Those who are cute are usually able to laugh at themselves, heartily, and draw you into the fun. This is not to say he is not romantic – far from it. It begins in the twinkle in his eye and quickly draws me into the seduction. Our lovemaking is magical – and real. There is no pretense or expectations. It evolves organically from the love we share, joyously and bubbles over any inconveniences that might arise. Thank you, all you women who overlooked this pearl among chaff for you have allowed me to uncover a gift beyond measure in the presence of my beloved, Jerry.

Health

Of course, this requires that we both bring our "A" game to the process. While not oblivious to our age, we refuse to accept the stereotypes society may have for our abilities and expected behaviors. We both treat our bodies with respect and are committed to taking good care to keep them healthy and in good shape so that we will be able to continue this dance together for many years hence.

I have learned to prepare more vegetables and fish and design meals that nourish not only our bodies but stimulate our senses. Jerry is refreshed by his daily several hour hikes in the red rocks which become more of a walking meditation for him. I prefer to meditate in my favorite chair.

We are learning more about the supplements we require to keep things working effectively as the natural processes in our bodies slow down and need additional support. An Integrative doctor and routine blood tests let us know how things are working and what we may need to supplement or stimulate production of the hormones that make things work the way God intended them to. We forgo most of the things that impede this process except on infrequent occasions and celebrations. All things in moderation. And we are committed to getting help for things that might not be working as well as we might wish. We owe that to each other. Life is good and we intend to keep it that way.

Hieros Gamos

You have come together to learn and demonstrate unconditional love and forgiveness so that you can move together into Hieros Gamos. There is no accident that you have united to make this possible. Your study and actions show that you have also transcended the difficult lessons that you came here to balance. The insensitivity, betrayals, and abandonment you inflicted before have been experienced and the karmic debts paid off in this one. Both of you have earned the right to experience the ecstatic joy of passion and compassion you are experiencing in the act of Hieros Gamos. As you come together, you will undoubted scratch the surface occasionally, injuring the tender skin around the thinly clothed heart. The balm of love can heal any wound if consciously applied. You are one who can do this. As you wear away your own rough edges, you will be able to lovingly and gently embrace this beloved and foster healing of his bruised heart in your tender care.

Mary Anna

Healing

Our dance together has many purposes. One of the most important is one of healing the wounds and actions we bring from previous lifetimes. In our intimate life together, we have the opportunity to experience the things we were unable to resolve then and have come back together to address.

While most of our actions together were glorious, there were occasions when I would say something in a tone of voice that turned him to stone and caused him to withdraw emotionally. Though there is no intention or awareness on my part, nevertheless, it causes discord that needs to be addressed consciously or it would derail the relationship. I asked Mother Mary Anna what was going on:

Soul Contracts

As you know, you have done this dance together in previous lifetimes. The fires were not the only things left smoldering. There were unresolved issues of control and direction that at times brought up impasses that you were unable to resolve. This is something you have come back together to address.

When Penny uses a voice of authority, it triggers a subconscious memory of a previous time when Jerry was powerless to protect himself and respond as he would have wished. Though that is not the case at this time, it is a subconscious issue that continues to bubble to the surface when you come together as closely as you are now doing. Penny's command of the situation was not always even handed in the past and Jerry felt unvalued and oppressed. He vowed to never let himself be manipulated like that again.

You bring up not only fears from this lifetime at the hands of his ex-wife but suppressed memories of the one before when he was at the mercy of your control. You were not always as loving as you are today and cared more for your selfish interests than the greater whole which he was part.

As for how you can deal with the situation today – we have a few suggestions:

1. Realize that this is an issue that you have come together to heal.
2. There are no right and wrongs. It is an on-going drama that is bringing these things to the surface for healing.
3. Step back from these encounters and look at the patterning that is being revealed. Does this interpretation represent the true reality of the situation with its motivations and intentions or is it just serving to bring to the surface these unhealed wounds for healing?
4. Look beneath the actions to the true character of the person you know in this lifetime. Does the situation at hand truly reflect the person you know he/she to be now? Have they moved through the previous lessons and are they now worthy of your forgiveness for past deeds?

5. *What are the feelings this is bringing up for me telling me about how I view myself in this moment as being able to chart my own destiny and be effective in my own life? Does this person or situation still control the events in my life, or have I moved through this pattern? Am I the director in my life and able to choose the responses I make, no matter what the actions of others?*

6. *What do I truly wish to create in my life? Do I believe I am worthy of the Loving journey together that is possible here or would I be more comfortable in a solo venture? Is it really about being comfortable or am I being asked to move past my comfort zone into a higher reality?*

7. *What is the lesson in love that this is showing me? Do I choose to live in fear or in love? Am I ready to let my fears control my life or do I wish to share a Loving path with this beloved? Is this someone I can trust to hold my heart in loving awareness?*

The journey together in incarnations is not an easy one but in the challenges comes the movement that elevates it to a higher form. You are both challenged to finding the loving path together, despite the illusions of the third-dimensional world. What do you Know to be true? Who do you trust to hold your hand in this walk together? Are you ready to continue on this divine adventure in love? If not now, when?

We share your concerns and hold you lovingly in our hands, knowing that whatever your choices, you are held in love and all is well.

Mary Anna

This began to make sense and put things into perspective. I know that in loving Jerry I am softening my presence in the world. I had developed a protective masculine shield that kept me safe from unwanted advances but also made it difficult for men to see the receptive feminine beauty I held within. The more I crack open this protective shell and surrender to his love, the more I allow this light to shine forth. I want to embrace the divine feminine aspects in my life for in doing so I encourage him to manifest more of the divine masculine in his. That is part of our journey together in Hieros Gamos.

Though he has assured me that he values my intelligence and ability to express myself verbally, I can see that this can be done more consciously. I have asked for his assistance in helping me become more aware of my actions by just raising his hand when I come on too strong or forcefully and it feels unloving. Both of us have a strong commitment to being loving and being loved. Anything that does not reflect this is jarring to the relationship. If we are mirrors to each other, it requires that we be honest when we experience something that does not reflect this. He is helping me grow in understanding and I believe I am helping him heal these wounds as well.

Communication

From the beginning Jerry and I have enjoyed communicating with each other with our voices as well as our bodies. While I came in as a Gemini under the ruling planet of Mercury, the sign of communication, which means it comes more effortlessly to me, this does not mean that I do not appreciate what he has to say. We both enjoy sharing our understandings and perceptions for in doing so we get to know each other even better. There is nothing we hold back from expressing just because we know that our partner does not share a similar perspective. We understand that by doing so, each from our unique vantage point in life, we both grow in understanding of the other and the world in which we live. It is said that marriage allows us to have two sets of eyes with which to see the world. How wonderful when we are able to share our perceptions with our beloved.

In the afterglow of our lovemaking, we frequently prompt the other to share the thoughts of love that this has ignited within us. It is in this intimate poetry of our soul we are able to hear the heart of the other, expressed in the words of the moment. As we gaze lovingly into each other's eyes, there is little doubt as to the sincerity of our thoughts, words, and actions which helps build a foundation of trust.

This has not always been easy. In the family in which I was raised, good-natured sarcasm was playfully used to complement each other by stating something so obviously untrue that it was ludicrous and humorous. This was not his experience and brought up painful and hurtful memories that caused him to shut down. By consciously sharing what this was bringing up for each of us to be healed, we were able to address this potential wound between us and move into a place of greater love and understanding. It is not so often what we say, but how it lands on the other's plate and the unconscious triggers it brings up for healing that is the real purpose of our dance together.

In previous relationships where I did not feel so heard and safe, I developed habits of non-verbal communication such as eye rolling. I am aware of this and have made a conscious effort not to go there since I do feel heard and appreciated in all ways.

Communication has been extremely important in our lovemaking. We are both verbally expressive and forthcoming about what feels good and what we like to share and receive. The more explicit we are in the words and how this is being experienced in our bodies, the more satisfying this is for both of us. Sharing with our Beloved our deepest feelings, concerns, and desires opens doors to the heart. If communication is the music of the dance of love, I am delighted that we are learning this melody together.

Balancing the Masculine and Feminine

Part of my dance with him is to soften the masculine side I have been reflecting for many years and learning to express my nurturing, receptive feminine nature. He is able to point out to me by the difference in my voice when I am in my masculine or feminine. While I am able to get a lot done in the masculine and have functioned quite well there in the past as a sovereign, this is not the role I wish to always play in this relationship. I enjoy the softer, nurturing feminine qualities that are flowering in me in our dance together. It also encourages him to step into his masculine in more meaningful ways. When I slip into a commanding stance it triggers feelings from instances where he felt a loss of personal power and control over his life. A hurtful prior marriage and uncaring bosses showed him the negative side of control rather than caring in relationships. We are together to reprogram that belief with love.

Time out

Occasionally our dance together becomes so intense we require time apart to process and reflect. I am glad Jerry decided to keep the RV in the desert where he can go for a few days and experience a little R & R and reconnect with the land in an environment that nurtures him. Sometimes it requires the distance of separation to see more clearly the things that are obscured in the fog of attraction. Without the distraction of his physical presence I can pray, meditate, channel, and get in touch with my inner guidance to see more clearly the choices and possibilities in my life. I can read, write, and commune with my soul to see more clearly the direction I wish to take. When we come back together, it is a joyful reunion where we are able to see our life together with a new perspective and rekindled desire.

Sacraments of Love

The Kiss

"Through the kiss we are born again. We give birth to each other through sharing of the love that is within us, blending God with the self. Through the sanctity of the kiss, two souls come together and merge as one. It is the prelude to the sacred union of the beloveds."

"The Kiss – the nashakh – the sacred kiss. Their souls merged through this sweet blending of the breath. No longer were they two, they were One." (The Book of Love by Kathleen McGowan)

From the beginning there has been something about our kiss that shifted paradigms. Jerry will tell you that it was like nothing he had ever experienced and disorienting to say the least. The shared breath that continues to draw us back into sacred expressions of love.

In his book *Journey of Souls,* Dr. Michael Newton talks about how in soul groups between incarnations we give each other sign so we will recognize each other. In this case it was also a kiss that continues to bind us one to the other.

"Those who recognize each other in this life in fullness that is unknowable to those who do not have this blessing?" (The Book of Love by Kathleen McGowan)

The Embrace

The average length of a hug between two people is 3 seconds. But researchers have discovered something fantastic. When a hug lasts 20 seconds, there is a therapeutic effect on the body and mind. The reason is that a sincere hug produces a hormone called "oxytocin", also known as the love hormone. This substance has many benefits in our physical and mental health, helps us, among other things, to relax, to feel safe and calm our fears and anxiety. This wonderful calming is offered free of charge every time we have a person in our arms, who cradled a child, we cherish a dog or cat, we're dancing with our partner, the closer we get to someone or just hold the shoulders of a friend.

This probably helps explain the euphoria and bliss we both feel when we hold and caress each other in the afterglow of our lovemaking. The more we prolong the embrace, the deeper we are drawn into the loving experience. Perhaps this is where the urgency of sex becomes the fully realized merging with the heart of the beloved as One.

Ten More Minutes

Mother Mary told me before we met that we would be reigniting a flame we had left smoldering from previous lifetimes. We had no idea that it would be so powerful. Neither Jerry nor I have ever felt such intense attraction before, even in our younger years. From the first time we embraced, we both felt an overwhelming energy that seemed sourced in a different reality. Rather than try to understand all of the forces at work here, we are just grateful for these intense feelings at this stage in our lives. Finding it difficult to part from our lovemaking, it became our joke to ask for "ten more minutes". No one ever told us that our "golden years" would be so fulfilling and exciting sexually.

Perhaps we are not only older but wiser in the workings of the body and patient in bringing together all of the elements to make things work well. The one thing that we have both found to elevate our lovemaking to a higher level is our total attention and focus on each other during all phases of our interaction. I am sure that fantasizing about another erotic reality might help some achieve a desired result, but it does not facilitate the higher, fully realized sexual experience we have come to appreciate. We are present with each other at every stage of our lovemaking and make it a point to engage each other visually and tune in to the eyes and facial expressions of our beloved as we pleasure each other in the acts of love. In doing so we become active participants as simultaneous givers and receivers of the sacraments of sexual expression as we bring loving energy alive in our bodies. The more we give, without expectation, the more we receive abundantly and are nourished in this mutual expression of *Hieros Gamos*.

We have made love literally hundreds of times and every time is new and exciting. Rather than coming in with a menu of who is to do what to whom and whose "turn" it is to receive, ours has become a co-creation of love expressed in the moment. There are no requirements or clocks in our sight. We come together in love and whatever evolves in this space is beautiful, loving and much deeper than just sex. Sometimes it is wildly passionate and expressive and others tender, sensual, and nurturing. Our movements are dictated by the knowing we feel by engaging not only the body but the soul of our beloved.

Our commitment to each other is to be sexually open to the other whenever there is the desire for nurturance and connection. We have always slept in the nude, usually in the embrace of the beloved. We easily fall asleep spooning in the arms of the other and are intimately nourished there throughout the night. Many times, one of us has reached out to the other in sleep and been welcomed into sexual embrace in a twilight state. Our favorite time is to wake in our lover's arms and to greet the day in mutual caressing, kissing, sucking, and fondling each other into an early morning lovefest. Making love in the afternoon is a gift of retirement that both of us appreciates. Neither of us has been this sexually expressive with others in our entire life but this whole experience as beloveds is beyond the third-dimensional experience and feels part of a new paradigm of loving expression.

We are not slaves to one form of sexual expression. Sometimes something may not be working as well as we might like. Fortunately, we have many things in our repertoire that can make the experience sexually fulfilling for both partners. It takes an openness to trying new things and finding out what really gives pleasure to our partner. If it takes a different position, approach, toy, inspiration, or motivation, that is part of the adventure and keeps things juicy and vibrant. It is an erotic dance being choreographed at a higher level.

"Sex can actually be a gateway through which spirit is accessed. Ken Wilbur (cited in Wade 2004: xi) adds: As the simplest, most accessible, most here-and-now transcendent experience that anybody can have, it is the most common doorway to the Divine, the most ordinary (in the best sense of the word) altered state that accelerates the stages of spiritual realization."

Ecstatic Union

Both Jerry and I are past the age when we are "supposed" to be having these incredibly sexual experiences, but we are. Never before in marriages or relationships has there been anything close to the intimate connection we are enjoying. It takes our breath away not only because of the intense physical attraction and expression, but the depth of our lovemaking it participates. Perhaps it is in "retirement" we have the time and knowledge to devote to the dance of love. Perhaps we know the value of selfless appreciation, truth, communication, openness, and devotion. The more we focus on honoring, and pleasuring the other, the more love is returned to us ten-fold. It elevates the entire experience to the level of bliss.

As Mary Anna has said *"You both, however unlikely given your age and prior experience, are living the possibilities of youthful erotic pleasure in the wisdom of experience. What could be more perfect? Continue to see the Light of God in your beloved's eyes and you will have even grander experiences in Hieros Gamos to come."*

As Mary Anna has suggested, we frequently share with our beloved our experiences in the expression of love. The words we speak share with our beloved how this is manifesting in our lives and our bodies. We read to each other inspirational books such as David Daida's *The Enlightened Sex Manual* and *Finding God Through Sex* so we understand how our bodies work and what we can do to be better sexual partners to our beloved and how to integrate this into an enlightened experience.

We make sure we are awake, and both fully engaged in each sexual experience, even if it is in the middle of the night. We take time to awaken each other sexually and are committed to whatever the other requires feeling desired, appreciated, and totally loved sexually. Afterward we hold each other tenderly and blissfully share the profound feelings that were revealed in our lovemaking.

"Hard Drugs"

One of the impediments to sexual expression at this age is frequently an inability of the male partner to achieve and maintain an erection. We were guided to use herbal supplements which our doctor says are safe and allows an erection at will for up to five days. Since he does not ejaculate frequently and deplete the sexual energy, we are able to repeat the experience as often as mutually desired.

Positions

Physical intimacy can take many forms. Physiology can direct the bodies to ways of coming together that provide the most pleasure and physical contact. We have found that the "woman on top" or "cowgirl" position is the most powerful for us in achieving not only deep penetration and sexual contact but allows us to experience more profoundly the experience of Hieros Gamos. This intimate communion of body, mind, and spirit finds full flowering as we move together in the ecstasy of the moment. Looking deeply into our beloved's eyes during the expression of our physical union becomes a joint celebration of the loving experience as One.

"As you two become One you will find God reflected in the eyes of your beloved and your beloved reflected in your own eyes." (The Book of Love by Kathleen McGowan)

Soaking Meditation

Jerry has limited experience meditating in the more conventional ways except in hiking which he regards as a walking meditation. While I have more experience in that arena, and can readily shift into a theta state, I have never found it helpful to focus on something with open eyes before. Studies have shown that gazing into your partner's eyes for four minutes a day can increase intimacy. We were guided to take our process of looking deeply into each other's eyes to a more profound level. This has become an especially healing and expansive experience for us as we share a bath or hot tub. The immersion and conductivity of this energy in a body of water elevates this experience to a sacrament of love that we both treasure and look forward to. As we gaze lovingly into our beloved's eyes immersed in this healing energy bath, the distractions of the outside world melt away and we are One in the experience.

This can begin with immersion of our bodies in the warm water, facing each other. This might be in a yab-yum position, at arm's length, or from opposite ends of the tub as long as you can look deeply into your beloved's eyes. You may wish to begin with a prayer, shared intention, or something you would like clarity on or just being in this loving space. As you focus lovingly into the windows to the soul of your beloved, you will find your breathing coming into synchronicity. The distractions of the mind and body become less intrusive as you see only their eyes and allow the intruding thoughts to melt away. There is no thought. It is not about making anything happen. It is not a sexual experience, though that energy will probably surface from time to time. It calls us to go deeper and feel for the seminal state that is calling for expression. The more one allows the urges to surface, be recognized, released, and dissipate in Loving awareness, the more you move deeper into the heart of love.

This might last the minimum four minutes but we find ourselves "blissing out" in the process and loosing track of time, until the cooling water draws us back into the present. Still in this sacred state, the "problems" and situations of our life are seen in greater clarity and we have the clearer perspective of the meaning and purpose behind our actions and inactions. The focus has shifted from our singular and separate concerns to the common vision of the relationship. We lovingly share our feelings, emotions, and perspectives this process has shown us. All of the concerns of the world may not have been solved but we are One in our approach to our life and love.

Seeing God in our Beloved

In the movie *Never Again*, Jill Clayburgh's character has trouble recalling the home of her new lover because when they were there before and made love "all she saw was God". That is what it may feel like when you really experience sacredness in physical union.

"When we are united with our beloved, we are living that love expressed and God is truly present in the bridal chamber. All love is God and God is all love".

"It is through our love together as humans that we find God. God is present in the bridal chamber when true beloveds are united. It is an ecstasy that touches divinity."

"Within the Hieros Gamos, the sacred union of the beloveds, God is present in their chambers. For a union to be blessed by God, both trust and consciousness must be expressed within the embrace. As the beloveds come together they celebrate their love in the flesh: they are no longer two but One. Outside the chamber they will live as love expressed in spirit." (The Book of Love by Kathleen McGowan).

*"We all taste God, taste Goddess, taste pure Spirit in those moments of sexual rapture, and wise men and women have always used that rapture to reveal Spirit's innermost secret. The very current of sexuality is plugged straight into God." (*Ken Wilber in the forward to *Finding God Through Sex* by David Daida)

For us, seeing God, Higher Power or whatever term is comfortable for you is about holding the light for each other to step into our divine blueprint and embrace the qualities that align us with our sacred selves. When we look lovingly into our beloved's eyes, we see only Love which is God.

Filip Coppens describes this: *"The primary purpose of the sacred marriage is that two equals, twin souls, a husband and wife, reunite through the Hieros Gamos. In short: The Hieros Gamos, or sacred marriage, was not a marriage of just any human beings, but of twin souls.*

The Hieros Gamos should therefore be more appropriately labelled the reunion of twin souls, while incarnate in the body, through sexual activity, involving the active participation of the male and female aspect of God: "What God has put together, let no man separate."

Those who have experienced such union find it largely impossible to describe – "beyond words". They are, however, capable of breaking down the experience in some components. During these encounters, the sexual activity exceeds – and is different from – a normal orgasm; it is normally more intense, prolonged and multiple, whereby the orgasm itself is more energetic, rather than physical. However, the presence of this divine energy should not be seen as a form of possession; normally, the human sexual energy is equally present, and the sexual experience is a balance and interplay between both energies.

It is also not so much ritual, but total union of body, mind and spirit: the two parts of one soul become united in the body, thus accomplishing in the body what they were at the beginning of time: a unity. The Great Work. And this union was "blessed" by the sacrament of the Hieros Gamos, in which God themselves, present at the separation of these souls at the beginning of time, reunited and blessed the two lovers.

Another person described it as "utter bliss" or what "heaven" must have felt like. The feeling of "heaven on earth" may indeed be what the Hieros Gamos was all about: the twin souls in heaven, experiencing their divine union on earth. As above, so below?" (Filip Coppens blog)

The Sacred Partnership we are creating requires utmost honesty, both with oneself and one's partner. Without this radical type of honesty, the Alchemy of Relationship cannot take place. It is the container of safety and appreciation that provides the reservoir for transformation. Until we had reached that level of honesty and total trust we were not able to access the true depth of sacredness in our relationship.

Mary Magdalene, as channeled by Tom Kenyon in his book with Judy Sion, **The Magdalen Manuscript – The Alchemies of Horus and the Sex Magic of Isis**, describes a process of accessing higher states of consciousness through specific sexual practices by which the Ka body (Egyptian term for the etheric double of the physical body or Taoist chi body) is activated. In this heightened ecstatic state, a magnetic field is created which catapults the beloveds beyond the mere physical act of sex into a seminal merging with the divine.

What makes Sacred Relationship sacred is that it is a truly a holy way of being. The root word of holy actually means to make whole. So, when we do something that creates wholeness (in this case psychological wholeness), we are engaged in a holy act.

"Essential to the female initiate (one who has chosen the sacred route) is the authentic feeling of safety and love or appreciation at the very least. When these are in place something within her being let's go and allows the alchemy to occur. The alchemy is created by the joining of the male initiate's Ka and the female initiates Ka. As they make love, the Ka bodies interconnect and this causes the female to open her magnetic floor" (the fundamental piece that has to occur).

"In the crucible of mutual safety, honesty and appreciation, it is possible to forge a new kind of self; a self with wings that can fly to places it could only imagine before. If these elements are in place within the relationship, the female can let go and allow the feminine mysteries to express through her. When this occurs during lovemaking, there is often a shuddering in the female. If she allows this to continue, it will take her deep into the mysteries.

If the male has trained himself to nest within the vibrational energies released by his partner, then both he and his Beloved can strengthen their Ka bodies. It is through the portal of nesting that the male initiate is able to enter the feminine mysteries of creation. When the Adoration of the Beloved occurs from both partners, the alchemy and Sex Magic greatly intensifies, for the harmonics and magnetics created by such emotion are very beneficial to the magic."

We found that many of the love-making rituals we enjoyed were, in fact, part of this process and created this elevated state of Hieros Gamos and expanded consciousness including:

1. Lovingly stroking, caressing, and massaging each other in in a way not necessarily focused upon the genitals, helps to awaken the passions and activate the endorphins and other chemicals of the body that transport us from our present state to open and build the magnetic fields where the magic takes place.
2. Because we feel love, safety, honesty, and appreciation from each other, we are able to open the inner portals of alchemy.
3. The building sexual energy is used to strengthen and elevate the Ka bodies where transformation is birthed. Ecstasy is food and nourishment for the Ka bodies.
4. We use the power of the breath and focus to move the energy within our bodies.
5. By gazing deeply into each other's eyes and being fully present in each other's experience, we create an intimate dance of common expression as One.
6. The movement of this heightened experience of energy exceeds anything we have ever experienced in ordinary genitally focused sexual expression.
7. Since by nature the male is electric in form and the female is magnetic in an alchemical sense, it is the nature of electricity to move and act while it is the nature of magnetics to enfold. When he surrenders into my embrace at the close of the intimate dance, we are able to merge the energies of our shared sexual experience and then curl or nest together into the bliss of the afterglow. The more we stay in this most intimate space, the closer we become and are able to move into deeper levels of love and appreciation.
8. In this state of total bliss, we fall naturally into a nesting or spooning position where our chakras align as One and we easily fall asleep in each other's embrace.

Jerry and I were overwhelmed by our elevated experience of Hieros Gamos. Nothing either of us has experienced before in our lives even comes close to this one of total immersion of self into One in this union. When we are "in the zone", totally connected physically, emotionally, and spiritually we move in concert with the divine. Far beyond normal orgasmic experience, we feel waves of ecstatic energy move through and around us, seemingly in a tube torus pattern that engulfs us both.   This brings unbelievable pleasure in waves, shudders, and release that repeat again and again as we connect with the eyes and the soul of our Beloved. This is utter bliss being experienced in form.

Commitment

It is our commitment to each other to love and be loved in the greatest measure we have ever known. We both are honored to share such love and are committed to sharing the blessed life we have been given for the rest of our days which we hope will be long. Our commitment is to hold each other in *Hieros Gamos*, the sacred marriage of the divine aspects of the masculine and feminine, in truth and consciousness. We will love, respect, and appreciate each other in kindness, caring, and compassion beyond experience or expectations. Our pledge to each other is to hold the other in an open palm knowing that we are together out of love and commitment not coercion, fear, or necessity.

We feel more "married" in spirit than we ever were in sanctified marriages. We do not rule out a ceremony at some point but that is not a requirement or high priority for us. We are One.

This was our feeling and commitment until five months into the relationship. Jerry came home from a brief trip to the desert and something had shifted. Gone were his reservations about the pain he associated with marriage, due to a debilitating previous marriage. It was a euphoric state that brought us closer together than ever. In the bliss of our reuniting he asked what my thoughts were on marriage. I said that while I did not require it, to me it indicated a deeper commitment and I was open to it. He asked me to be his wife and I accepted. We had an exciting time visioning what that would mean to our lives and how we might plan a future together.

Healing Wounds

Part of our journey together in *Hieros Gamos* is to heal wounds. His experiences in the prior marriage were excruciating. Slowly the feelings of fear and flashbacks of his previous experiences in marriage began to surface. He withdrew and became despondent feeling that he had made a commitment he could not fulfill. Though he realized that I was "not even the same species" as his former wife and none of the things she had done were in my repertoire, he was overtaken with grief and was reliving these old traumas.

Flower and Gem Essences

Depression is something I am familiar with. My late husband and I both studied flower essences at Findhorn and had our own flower and gem essence company for many years. He suffered from chronic depression before we were married. Doctors said this was from a chemical imbalance and he would be on medication for the rest of his life. Through a protocol of flower and gem essence therapy we were able to cure the depression and it did not recur. After a year of taking the essences every day, he had removed all of the mental, physical, emotional, and spiritual imbalances that had created the depressive state and never had to take them or medication for depression again.

I asked Mother Mary Anna and the Deva of Flower Essences if I should put together a flower and gem essence remedy for Jerry and they helped me do so. I just asked what he needed, and they gave me the ones to address things that were beyond my awareness. As

I looked up the meaning of the different essences they recommended, a picture emerged of what was being brought up:

Aquamarine - for fear, stress and anxiety.

Banana – stills the mind and helps us be fearless about the past, present, and future.

Blue Spruce – Helps those renegotiating priorities and life focus.

Brazilian Quartz – Realigns chakras. Cleansing white light energizes and synchronizes the auric field.

Fluorite – Clear focus of issues coming for healing at this time.

Star of Bethlehem – for dealing with grief, depression, sorrow, despondency. To comfort and sooth the pain.

I prepared the remedy and he began taking it in water throughout the day. I told him that I was there to love him unconditionally and a marriage commitment was not relevant to that or necessary. I was committed him and to his health – physical, emotional, mental, and spiritual and would do anything I could to assure that he was happy and healthy.

We canceled the "wedding ring" we had ordered because this was definitely going to be a different kind of a union. One day at a time…

Depression

Depression is an insidious state that keeps us from seeing love in ourselves, our partners, and our lives. As I had experienced this with my late husband, I was able to recognize the symptoms that were surfacing in the safety of our relationship for healing. The dark clouds of depression prevent our seeing the light of love in our beloved's eyes. My challenge was to continue to hold that light for both of us until he had moved through this state. He went through the motions of life but gone was the spark of love that had animated our dance together. I continued to reassure him throughout the day that I was there in love, even though he could not perceive it. He was unable to express his love for me in return because he had lost all connection to that feeling.

Frequently it requires bringing up all of the deep insecurities and misconceptions that do not resonate with the loving presence that we are that is most painful. But until we allow these to surface, the wounding will only be covered over on the surface but continue to fester within, only to erupt more virulently later. He had to suffer this "dark night of the soul" in order to purge these contaminants from his being.

Our challenge as beloveds is to allow this process to take place and to hold their hands s they heal. We are tempted to "fix" the other but unless this is their shift in perception, it will be us doing the heavy lifting and preventing their growth into awareness. It is like shining a light in a dark cellar and seeing the rats that scurry away. I was there unflinchingly to hold the light and help guide him through the darkness, back into the light, reminding him that I loved and cared for him always, unconditionally.

He continued to ingest the essences throughout the day. I was guided to put the essences into massage oil along with essential oils of rose and lavender. I massaged these into his body as he relaxed into the nurturing sensation of love and caring being received into every pore of his being. He rested peacefully and in the morning, rolled over, looked deeply into my eyes and told me he loved me. His soul was resurfacing from the darkness...

A week by himself in his RV in the desert and he came home numb and empty. He had purged many of the old beliefs and fears that were part of his old paradigm. I began to help him refill with love. Flower essences and another massage began to imprint this new reality in his mind and body. It was like watching a light that had almost gone out flicker back to brightness and become stronger. First the joy in our lovemaking returned. Then his awareness and concern for the world around us...

Inspirational movies began kindling sparks of awareness and remembrance of long-forgotten dreams and intentions that had been buried by the minutia of life lived in semi-darkness. It was like waking up from a long sleep and finding that the sun had come out and there were people with the same dreams and visions that were intent on creating a new reality. He began doing extensive research to see what others had been doing and where he might fit in and contribute to this new paradigm of truth and consciousness and how we might walk this path together. It was a step up into a higher dimension of consciousness where the individual concerns of the ego were no longer paramount, and the greater picture of Oneness was coming into view. We began to envision a future together in loving service.

Continuing the process... Healing is like removing the layers of an onion; as one issue is brought into awareness and healed, the next layer surfaces for attention. The first round of flower essences removed many blocks and signs of depression and restored feelings of loving energy between us, but there were still times when I felt him slipping back into a shell of emptiness. By spending hours researching the atrocities of man in order to see the things that need re-visioning, he became more and more despondent. It was time to prepare a new flower remedy.

By connecting with the Deva of Flower and Gem Essences and the Deva of Healing I was able to formulate another tincture to help him in his healing process. They recommended:

Rhodolite Garnet for emotional disconnected from parts of the body that are in pain. It helps reconnect with parts of the body that have been traumatized and rebuilds the web of etheric energy.

Topaz for when you are unable to take decisive action that supports one's true self. It clears energy blockages in the 3rd chakra and strengthens the ability to act decisively from a clear sense of personal identity.

Star of Bethlehem for the effects of shock from childhood and a previous marriage. Comfort for the sense of emptiness and feelings of loss.

Orange for enthusiasm, energy, and banishing melancholy.

Control vs. Concern and Caring

As we come together as One in divine partnership, it is frequently as two animals in a sack, each struggling to see where they leave off and the other begins. Where before we had boundaries and sovereignty over our actions, this concept is blurred in the intimacy of the partnership. The caring concern of one partner can easily be misconstrued as an attempt at control if there is not trust and consciousness. If one has never experienced true love and caring, the sudden infusion of this gift into the relationship can cause the newbie to recoil in protection from something they interpret as an attempt to control. Note how the mere act of preparing an unexpected meal for the beloved could be misconstrued as trying to control the diet of the other if there is not this level of acceptance and appreciation that they are unused to. This is also part of the dance of Hieros Gamos.

Flower essences are gentle catalysts for change and awareness. As they work they bring to the surface the old wounds and misperceptions for healing and release. It would be easy to judge the fears and emotions that surface by third-dimensional perspectives. However, we chose to take a different approach. The sacred union of Hieros Gamos is celebrated by gifting the other with mirrors which symbolizes our commitment to the other to be honest reflections. Instead of taking the insecurities that surface as a personal affront, we are encouraged to look within our own perceptions to see how we are coming off to the other and what we can learn about ourselves from the process without blaming or attacking them. Instead of reacting immediately to his insecurities and personal concerns about freedom in the relationship I took a "time out" to see how my own insecurities and perceptions were mirroring his.

As Don Miguel Ruiz states in *The Four Agreements*, we can avoid a lot of drama if we "don't take anything personally" and "don't make assumptions". It all comes down to honest communication. We are blessed in that we are both committed to sharing our feelings, apprehensions, concerns, and reactions so that we get the reflection of our soulmate for clarity. Difficult as it may be, by doing so, we are less likely to read things into the other's actions that were not intended or to misinterpret something that is ours for the learning.

I had decided to house and dog sit for my sister in a different state for three weeks while she was vacationing. I wanted Jerry to come with me and he did not. I was sad and disappointed because I had assumed wrongfully that he would want to go because I did. We had a long talk about it, each expressing what were our own personal needs and desires and why we wished the other would do what we wanted them to do.

I finally realized that my imposing my will upon him would only put him in a place of resentment rather than peace. I wish only peace and love between us. I may choose to be sad because he will not be with me, but he knows that I respect his sovereignty and honor that he was willing speak up and do what he knew what was right for him rather than acquiesce to my desires. I thought that it would be a lonely three weeks, but I was hopeful that we would both come back together nourished and refreshed.

Honeymoon

As time came for me to go drew closer, we became more aware of what it would mean to be apart for three weeks. I was resigned that I would go by myself and made no effort to convince or manipulate him otherwise. He continued to take the flower essences and slowly came to the realization that he did not want us to be separated either. He rose above his concerns and said he would like to go with me. I was overjoyed.

Three weeks in a beautiful place with time to really experience each other without the distractions of "life" became a honeymoon that brought us closer and closer. And that is where the fear began to set in.

When we returned he said he needed a break and returned to his RV home in the desert. Days became weeks as he struggled with the concept of spending the rest of his life in a "marriage", sanctioned or otherwise. His prior experiences had shown him that it could be stifling and demoralizing, but could he trust that this was different? There he was in a community where he was valued and nurtured and felt that he had a useful purpose. He did not know how to create that same experience in a relationship with me, a powerful and self-actualized woman.

I struggled as well. How could he not realize the magnificence of the love we had experienced and want to extend that into eternity? I had the advantage of inner knowing and "friends in high places" who continued to tell me that this was a divine assignment, but he must be willing to step into that experience as well. "If only" he would come back he would remember the intense energy of love we experienced together that elevated us into the experience of Hieros Gamos…

The experience of Hieros Gamos is so intense and all-encompassing that it can be frightening if you continue to view love through the rear-view mirror of past third-dimensional experiences. Real caring can be misinterpreted as control. Without self-love, one will not feel worthy of this exalted experience. Immersion into the One requires that we release the garments we have clothed ourselves in to protect us from the pains of growth. He had told me that no one had ever loved him as I did. That was part of the "problem". He did not know how, or at least was not ready, to receive that love and move into this new paradigm.

He faltered… He told me that he was an old man (68!) and just wanted a peaceful, uneventful life. That did not seem to be what I would be bringing to the relationship. He was happy in the desert and did not want to move to Sedona. He knew I would shrivel in the confines of the limited possibilities in the desert. We were at a stalemate.

As I waited for Jerry to "come to his senses" I began to examine my own and what I had learned so far from our journey together. Michael Mirdad talks about the importance of personal boundaries. It is about self-respect, self-nurturing, and loving yourself enough to say no.

Sometimes we come together with our soulmates for a lifetime, and sometimes just to share a lesson. It is all good because it is all part of God's ever-unfolding fabric of life. Our charge is to show up in love in every aspect of our lives and let the mystery reveal itself.

Namaste, my beloved…

Mother Mary Anna continued to reassure me that this was in divine order.

You are fully aligned with the new paradigm and have set an unwavering course to that destination. Jerry is still a bit wobbly since he does not see this as clearly defined as you do. Not to worry. When all of the pieces fall into place, he will be there as your protector and defender that will help facilitate your path together. He is merely collecting all of his forces so he does not feel so scattered and will be able to move with meaning and purpose when the time is right.

While Jerry has not seen how he will fit in there yet, rest assured that he is an integral part of that environment. Allow him to move into that space without any coercion on your part and he will feel it is his choice rather than your directive. That is the key...he has to want to be with you and not feel that you are commanding his presence. **He either shows up fully or you are not weighed down by his presence**. *Decision time but things bode well since you have kindled important fires together.*

Mary Anna

Decisions

From somewhere in the ethers I received the following message:

You are on the precipice surveying the road ahead without a roadmap. Only your soul knows the trajectory of each path.

On one hand you can lie peacefully in your grave waiting for the sands of time to slowly cover you grain by grain. This is a slow process that can take 30 years if you do not become restless and move to higher ground. The last years will not be pleasant but this is the price you will pay for non-involvement in the world you came here to help change.

The other route is steeper and more challenging but the rewards and possibilities for growth greater. The vistas and adventures as the consort of the goddess are breathtaking and ultimately less challenging for they follow a shortcut to eternity with a soul guide and partner in the experience. Certainly, there are potholes, but they are there to guide you onto higher ground. Together you have the resources to make the journey joyful if indeed both are traveling in a tandem of commitment and consciousness. Near the end is an escalator that bypasses the infirmities that prolong other journeys. This is a one-way ticket with a transfer at the finish so that you can move to the next level.

Which do you choose?

Stunned by the clarity of the situation I shared it with him without comment and let go.

Jerry Retrograde!

Sedona has powerful energy and is known to shake worlds upside down as we realign with our higher soul's purpose. Jerry did not want to go to New Mexico but did not know how to tell me so. He still did not feel comfortable in my environment. Given his past experiences in love, he did not want to repeat the pattern, but did not trust himself to do things differently.

He retreated into hermit mode in the desert and immersed himself back into the environment where he did not feel challenged and was appreciated. Days turned into weeks, weeks into months with only an occasional e-mail wishing me well and sending love to me and our friends.

At first I was blindsided and felt that the rug of my world had been pulled out from under me. Here was the most loving man I have ever known, turning his back on all that I was offering him! What had I done wrong? What did I need to sacrifice of me in order to have love in my life? I examined what my actions might have unconsciously conveyed to him and reevaluated what was really important in my life.

Gradually I began to change – for me – and not to fit into any imagined mold of what I thought he wanted. I decided to stay in Sedona was where I was nurtured on multiple levels and began a circle of women to help us grow and create a new paradigm of association together based on loving awareness. We practiced making each other feel loved, honored, and respected. I became the loving presence I was looking for in a partner but made no effort to find another.

In the womb of the desert, he had the distance to process the things in his life that he needed for his growth as well. He tried sky diving and realized he wasn't afraid anymore. He fixed broken things and became "useful" to those who also found solace in that isolated environment. He bought a monster truck to restore and play in to distract him from the loneliness but soon realized it was not enough. Finally, he came to understand that he really did deserve more than he was settling for in the desert and began to love himself enough to go for it.

Jerry Direct

After seven months Jerry finally came to the realization that all he ever loved and wanted was waiting for him in Sedona if only he could restore the connection. Tentatively he sent an e-mail inviting me to share a dinner with him on his upcoming birthday. I responded that I would be delighted, without demands, admonishments, or expectations. That led to a lengthy phone call and arrangements to spend the holiday weekend together.

Our time apart had given us the opportunity to reflect on our lives with more perspective and greater clarity. We both realized that the deep love we have for each other is sacred, holy, and unaffected by the growth we each needed to step to the next level in the relationship. Painful as it was, we had both grown and matured in the experience. We both realize the extraordinary gift and grace of Hieros Gamos in our lives and the gift of love we are able to share through such a profound sexual connection. Fears were gone as well as the "requirements" we had placed on each other to be anything other than the loving partners we are. We slipped seamlessly back into Oneness, wiser, and better prepared to weather the storms of life. We began planning a new life together committed to consciously holding each other in love....

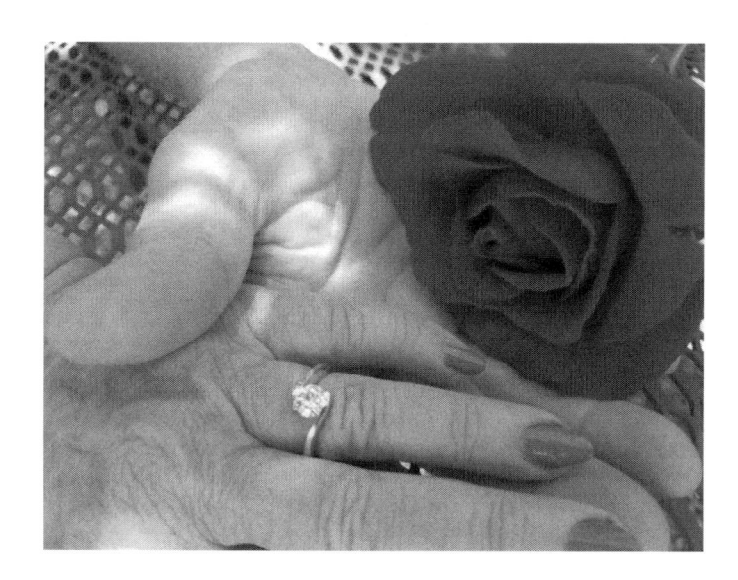

*God is love and we are made in God's Image! Our job then, is to act like it. We are here to love God and each other (including ourselves) AND live a life of loving service. (*Michael Mirdad*).*

Lighting the Way for Others

As you come into resonance with your beloved, you will begin to realize the purpose of your journey together. You will see where your experiences overlap and where the voids are, waiting to be filled in. As you process the minutia of everyday life, you will also begin to see the perfection of the association. This is a gift to each other that is divinely orchestrated for your growth and understanding but also for others on the path.

Now all gifts are not necessarily perceived as such from the beginning. Undoubtedly there will be things that "rub you the wrong way" about your partner in this experience. Your challenge and opportunity is to look beneath this irritation to discover the thorn that is piercing an old wound, waiting to be healed. The more of these subterranean irritants you can explore with your beloved, the clearer will be the field for your work together.

Now we say work, though it will seem more like play when you are both doing things that nourish your soul. You are being called to clear your field and refine your dance together so that you can mirror this to others. Part of the awakening that is taking place calls for those who "get it" at the seminal level of enlightened service to share this light energy with others. Together you are beacons that will shine brightly in a world of darkness. You are to be mirrors, not just to each other, but to those in your sphere of influence that are looking for new role models in a world of distorted images of what it really means to be fully evolved representations of masculine and feminine. Those who are anomalies and are the most repugnant in their ignorance are frequently those who get all the press. We intend to alter that by giving brighter lights to those who are more evolved representatives of the divine masculine and divine feminine. These are the ones who will be the role models in the new paradigm.

So how do you go about becoming a brighter light to those around you? We might suggest that the journey begins with becoming comfortable with yourself, your relationship, and how this is evolving in the world. You must have trust in yourself and your beloved as well as the firm connection to God who is the third partner. There must be willingness by both to "come out" and share openly and earnestly the struggles, awakenings, and revelations in their journey together in order to inspire others to do the same. Any false bravado or ingenuineness will be detectable and counterproductive to the process.

You must also realize that by opening yourself to the world, there will be no hiding of the shadow. The more you are able to heal and reveal the struggles in your journey together, the more you empower others to do the same. If you are to be role models, it is because you have doubts, frailties, and shortcomings like others, but you are able to mirror how you have moved through these together and used them as opportunities for growth and understanding.

This is a journey in tandem but also as a pebble that causes great radiating waves of understanding if you choose to share your journey with others. The messages we are sharing with you are so profound and revolutionary when compared with the expression of "love" in your modern culture that there are sure to be backlashes. The modern conception of love and marriage frequently is of such a low vibration that it might be compared as organized competition where none are the victors. We wish to alter that paradigm and give visions and glimpses of possibilities for a union that honors not only each other, but their divine journey together.

You can be missionaries in this process if you choose to go there with us. When you and your beloved feel aligned and in tune with your divine center, you are ready to begin to share this with others. Perhaps you may wish to begin with friends who have noticed the glow of your partnership. Perhaps this will expand to discussion groups with those who are on a similar path.

As you begin to increase your confidence and vibration you may wish to hold workshops and seminars where you bring this expanded way of being together to a wider audience. These are the sparks of light that will ignite a bonfire of awareness if done honestly and consciously. Be willing to work together to this common purpose and you will honor the commitment to your soul's journey together.

Namaste, Mary Anna

Pass it On

As to where you might go with this, we have a few suggestions:

First, it is important to realize that your journey together is in divine order. It is no accident that you have come together on a spiritual path of discovery. It is an agreement you made prior to incarnation to meet and take each other to this higher level of understanding. And it is meant to be joyful.

Second, we might wish to point out that this is all about growth and appreciation. The more you learn to appreciate the unique gifts you bring to each other and the perfection of the dance, the more you will grow in understanding of the process.

Third, this is a unique opportunity for self-exploration in the eyes of your complement who has volunteered to be the mirror you require for this adventure together. If you are able to use this for self-reflection and see the lessons and the triggers as your wake-up call, reflected in their eyes, the greater will be not only your growth and understanding but the elevation of the vibration of yourselves and the collective.

This journey together is meant to be one of joy and wonder. The ecstasy of being in total communion with the beloved of your soul's longing is one of the seminal moments of earthly existence. It is by extending this moment each day by conscious adherence to the process we have given that you will create the heaven on earth of your desires.

As with the loaves and fishes, you have an over-flowing abundance of God's love created through this union to share with others. Be the channel and creator of this energetic flow to all in your sphere of influence and you will be of great service to humanity. This is the charge of your soul, to be love in the arms of your beloved and to pass it on. In so doing you become one with the divine. Welcome Home. Mary Anna

Finally

As you come into divine harmony with your beloved we would like to remind you that this is not a solo journey merely for your enjoyment. There is a greater process taking place utilizing the pattern of Hieros Gamos as its guide. The reawakening of the divine aspects of the masculine and feminine is for many the beginning of the process of reunification into your divine pattern. While this is necessary and far-reaching in its implication, it is the key to the lock of higher awareness.

As you merge into the union of partnership and coalescence into unified purpose and commitment to the other and the divine, you will begin to move together in divine harmony in all aspects of your life. This common vision and purpose will undoubtedly involve expansion into a greater community of souls embarking upon a similar path. This is a coming together of a gathering of Christed beings that have ears to hear and have heeded the call into Oneness. While not moving en masse into the ethers, there will nevertheless be a disbursal into corners of the world that can use the example of what it means to take this next step into growth and awareness. Yours is a light and a witness through your actions, as well as your words, of the transformation that is taking place through love in a world on the brink of darkness. This is a message that must be heard and those with ears to hear are being called to magnify this to others.

Your mission, if you choose to accept it, is to love one another to the fullest extent of your being and to pass it on. Simple as this may sound, it is in the understanding and the follow through that things get sticky. However, we have given you the guidelines and requirements to make this happen. While this is most effective in partnership with a beloved, that is not entirely necessary for it to occur. What is required is to become this awareness and presence within yourself, thus radiating this energy to all in your sphere of influence. It is about altering the energetic environment of the planet through conscious application of love on a grander scale. The more souls you bring into this vibrational frequency, the more you plant the seeds that will take root and spread. Become the "Johnny Appleseed" of love and you will leave a lasting impact on the world around you.

As for your dance with your beloved, we might suggest that you read study and discuss the processes we have given you together. This will require constant reinforcement until the principles are mastered. It requires total honesty and commitment to each other and the relationship for as long as you continue to love and grow together. While there can be more than one conscious divine union in a lifetime, once this perfection is achieved, there is little incentive to go elsewhere unless the dynamics change drastically. All is required is for you to continue to work together in total truth and honesty and trusting that all is working in divine order since God is also part of this triumvirate. That is the key. When the ego wrests the controls away, the partnership can derail off the track Home.

We bless you and your journey together. The greatest gift of your divine Father is the promise of fulfillment and ecstasy found in your beloved's arms. Together you are held in the hand of God...
Much Love, Mary Anna

New Ceremonies of Commitment

Just as our concept of loving relationships and marriage are changing, so must be the ceremonies that honor and celebrate these life-altering events. We came to realize that the reason we were having trouble with the whole idea of "marriage" is that the way it is usually celebrated and misused in our third-dimensional world is no longer relevant for us in the new paradigm we are creating.

Once again I went to Mother Mary Anna and asked for her insight and assistance in creating a ceremony that celebrates and honors the commitment to Hieros Gamos.

Mother Mary Anna on Sacred Union Ceremonies

My dearest Penny,

You have indeed picked up the theme that we alluded earlier that the ceremonies of the old paradigm are no longer valid in this new reality. While many couples are approaching the subject with more clarity and respect than their parents did, there clearly is much lacking if we are to use the yardstick of the higher concepts of love and commitment. Your traditional marriage ceremonies are still founded upon patriarchal principles and attempt to bind one to another under the authority of laws of church and government rather than by fostering love and trust. Is it any wonder that so many marriages are unable to maintain this standard and fall apart or remain in name only without the loving attention that drew them together in the first place?

We would like to suggest that it might be time to create celebrations reflective of the higher nature of spiritual partnerships and the reasons for their formation. While there will always be marriages that codify responsibilities and issues relevant to procreation, that has little meaning for those who come together for reasons of the heart that do not require the strong arm of the law to enforce fidelity or maintenance. Even those are becoming less effective in your diverse society.

We would encourage you to look deeper at the meaning and purpose of reuniting the masculine and feminine aspects of God. It is certainly a prime directive that has been part of the divine plan from the beginning. Where it might have been of economic and physical necessity at one time, in the new paradigm both are self-sufficient, independent beings that somehow must find a loving path together. So, what are the reasons these conscious souls might wish to come together in partnership?

Certainly, they have a natural affinity for each other that is part of the magnetic nature of their being that draws them into union with their complement. This is of course physical, but there is also a "magnetic" programming wired into our psyche that is looking for the other half of our soul that knows and understands us and in whom we feel complete.

Part of the adventure of the new paradigm is the dynamic growth that takes place when soulmates come together to uplift, support, and encourage each other on their spiritual path. The contracts that were made on the soul level before incarnating are there to guide our journey together even though the path may be unconscious.

Soulmates are indeed mirrors to each other of both our shadow and our light so that we can use their reflective abilities to "clean up our act" and grow together into our divine qualities. We say divine qualities because even though we are created in God's image, often we do not embrace this image and cloak ourselves in darkness, so we do not see this holy aspect of ourselves. Our soulmate has "x-ray vision" and is able to see past this subterfuge into the soul ready to blossom. It is our challenge to help them reveal this beauty and allow their inner radiance to shine forth in our tender embrace.

So, does this require the approval of church or state if the couple are conscious adults, committed to truth? We think not, but that is up to the couple to determine. If they need the reminder, approval, and boundaries set by society to remain on the evolutionary path, then perhaps marriage offers that structure. However, if the recognized purpose of the relationship is to explore and experience love in its most profound state, an official document is unnecessary.

This comes back to the ceremony of commitment. We would like to suggest that those that are embarking upon a life together on this higher path might wish to codify their commitment to each other in a different way. The understanding and support of a partner and a nurturing society can be important in traversing this new terrain together. If one knows that those in their circle of intimates (whether or not it is nuclear family) are part of this grand adventure, it can be easier to stay the course together. If there is a commitment witnessed by a soul family, it brings all together as part of this grand adventure into love. When things get sticky in the dance with the beloved, it is the congregants who have witnessed and affirmed this loving partnership that are the first line of support in seeing the larger picture and the common path. In effect all who are part of the ceremony of the heart become part of the adventure together and are not just witnesses but participants in this dance of love.

In the ceremony of commitment, it should be stated the purpose of the sacred union and why the beloveds have chosen to take this step in declaring their love and commitment to the community. This is a new concept to many, and part of your challenge is to help educate the participants in the event that is taking place. This is a group dance and the beloveds have chosen to be the instigating partners that begin this new paradigm together.

The declarations by the participants are about inspirations, intentions, promises, and commitments in the expression of love. It affirms to themselves and those present how they intend to show up in each other's lives and within the community. This is a contract between the beloveds and God and the participants are witness to this. It is neither required nor implied that this has any legal relevance or stature.

As the beloveds share their commitment to be ministers of love to each other, they in turn will pass on this charge to those in their circle of intimates. This is a divine assignment to love one another and is passed on in loving awareness to those in attendance. In that all are One. And so it is...

Mary Anna

In the New Relationship Paradigm

"This year the focus will be on first waves embodying the new template of The Hieros Gamos, (the sacred marriage union with our divinity), and the complete change it will require in all human intimate relationships. It will have a significant impact within the current reality system around "legal" or "religious" marriages. Many people on the planet have been or will end significant relationships, such as marriage, or transition through them into higher expressions of spiritual union or meet their next relationship partner and get married. This marriage may be considered legal or not, however it indeed will be a spiritual agreement. The result of this new Hieros Gamos template included in the planetary mind/logos means that marriages and all relationships will be significantly impacted. The level of inner balance and spiritual and emotional maturity that you have accepted, will reflect your relationship work with your inner self and the "spiritually assigned" relationship partner.

The Hieros Gamos is revealing itself to be manifested as a sustained holographic re-patterning and re-education program designed for achieving inner and outer sacred marriage through self-focused healing and spiritual empowerment. It is designed to connect then unify God Source with all levels of identity and their human relationships. Sacred Marriage is a state of being in our hearts that we have desperately missed and have been yearning for since the beginning of time.

For many of us on the spiritual and ascension pathway, it has been a difficult, solitary and lonely journey. This Hieros Gamos template has been birthed through the result of the devoted and diligent work of many, many Lightworker's during the Ascension cycle.

Lisa Renee Jones

A Ceremony of Sacred Union

All congregants receive an unlit votive candle.

From *The Poet Prince* by Kathleen McGowan:

In the book called Genesis, this told as Adam's twin being created from his rib, which is to say his own essence, as she is flesh of his flesh and bone of his bone, spirit of his spirit.

Then God said, "And they shall become as one flesh."

Thus, the Hieros Gamos was created, the sacred marriage of trust and consciousness that unites the beloveds into one flesh. This is our highest gift from our father and mother in heaven. For when we come together in the bridal chamber, we find the divine union that El and Asherah wished for all their earthly children to experience in the light of pure joy and the essence of true love.

And from the Legend of Solomon and Sheba by Kathleen McGowan:

Solomon was mightily taken by Makeda's beauty and presence and disarmed in total by her honesty. The wisdom he saw in her eyes reflected his own, and he knew immediately that the prophets were correct. Here was the woman who was his equal. How could she be else, when she was the other half of his soul?

And it was then that the Queen of Sheba and King Solomon came together in Hieros Gamos, the marriage that unites the bride and the bridegroom in a spiritual matrimony found only within divine law. The Goddess of Makeda blended with the God of Solomon in a union most sacred, the blending of the masculine and the feminine into one whole being.

They stayed in the bridal chamber for the full cycle of the moon in a place of trust and consciousness, allowing nothing to come between them in their union, and it is said that during this time the secrets of the universe were revealed through this union. It is said that Solomon had many wives, yet there was only one who was a part of his soul. While Makeda was never his wife by the laws of man, she was his only wife by the laws of God and nature, this is to say the law of Love. (The Poet Prince by Kathleen McGowan)

Within the Hieros Gamos, the sacred union of the beloveds, God is present in their chambers. For a union to be blessed by God, both trust and consciousness must be expressed within the embrace. As the beloveds come together, they celebrate their love in the flesh; they are no longer two, but One. (The Book of Love by Kathleen McGowan)

We surrender our egos and our hearts into each other's keeping that we might be forever joined in love and tenderness, surpassing all bounds and fetters. As we come together in this sacred union of Hieros Gamos we sanctify the holy state of this relationship and our devotion to it and to each other.

I gift to you my beloved this symbol of our twin souls coming together once again in time, united by the brilliance of our eternal love.
The giving of the ring(s).

As the grail barer I share with you my knowing that we may drink together from the cup of knowledge and grow together in love and understanding.

The sharing of the chalice

This sacred cord, the *cordeliere,* symbolizes the joining of two hearts for eternity. It is wound gently around the wrists and tied loosely together.

I surrender myself to your love to be held not by earthly binding but by the heart strings that we play as One.

I hold you gently in my heart, knowing that we are bound for eternity not by the laws of man but through the sanctity of our love.

And they say together from the poem of Maximus:

I have loved you before.
I love you today.
And I will love you again.
The time returns.
And the *cordeliere* is unwound.

In your reflection, you will find what you seek. As you two become One, you will find God reflected in the eyes of your beloved, and your beloved reflected in your own eyes. (from The Book of Love by Kathleen McGowan, p318)

There is an exchange of hand mirrors.

We gift to each other these mirrors as reminders that we are here to mirror truth to each other, unflinchingly so that we may heal and grow together as love personified.

I promise to be an honest reflection to you and to help you see your own divine nature through my eyes.

All love is God and God is all love.

When we are united with our beloved, we are living that love expressed and God is truly present in the bridal chamber.

The song begins with a kiss, for this is the most sacred form of expression between the beloveds. In our holiest tradition that comes from Solomon and Sheba, the word is nashakh, *and it means more than simply to kiss; it means to breathe in harmony in a way that combines the spirit of two into one, to share the same breath, to blend the life forces in a single coming together.*

Through the kiss we are born again. We give birth to each other, through the sharing of the love that is within us, binding God with the self.
Through the sanctity of the kiss two souls come together to merge as one. It is the prelude to the sacred union of the beloveds. (The Book of Love by Kathleen McGowan).

We celebrate this union with the kiss, the sharing of the sacred breath experienced by beloveds.

The beloveds kiss.

Our commitment to each other is to love and be loved.
Our commitment to the community is to mirror that love to you.
The beloveds each take their individual candles from the altar and light together the candle of Hieros Gamos.

In the coming together of these two lights there is created a conflagration of greater intensity that extends into the community where the light of love is birthed and experienced. We invite you all to bring your candles and light them from the candle of Hieros Gamos so that you can be part of this loving experience and claim it for your own. Please place your candle in a container and return with it until all have been lit.

Repeat together: *We bless each other,*
in this light of love,
that it might rekindle the divine spark,
of love in the hearts of all.

With my body I thee worship
And with all my worldly goods I thee endow.

Please take these candles home with you when you go to remind yourself of this commitment to love and be loved. For now, you may place them around the room when we are through.

For no longer are you two, but you are one in spirit and in flesh. And what God has put together, let no man separate.

And so, it is...

Postscript:

Jerry and I were together four years to the day and were able to experience the ecstasy of love lived to the fullest in Hieros Gamos.

On the Ides of March 2019, he told me that while he loved me deeply and thought I was a "awesome woman", he was not happy and fulfilled living with me and my adult son in Sedona. He had decided to move back to the small town in the Arizona dessert where he resonated with the people and the lifestyle and had plenty of work to keep him busy. He had struggled in Sedona to fill his days with things that utilized his talents. We both knew I would be miserable there. While he dutifully participated in activities in my world, he had made no attempt to cultivate other friendships or involve himself in community activities. It seemed our journey together was over.

I was blindsided and although I loved him and was prepared to spend the rest of our lives together, I knew on a deep level that we were quite different, and my life was not fulfilling for him. I also know that unconditional love means wanting the best for the other, despite how it might affect you personally. We lovingly parted and within a week he had moved out of my home and my life...

As is my practice I went to Mother Mary Anna and asked for her perspective on the situation...

When Jerry came into your life, I said that it would be to rekindle old fires and he did that. He also helped you remove some of the barbs that were preventing you from experiencing the full flowering of loving expression. You did much for him and awakened him to that experience. He will now know how to recreate that in all of his relationships and has you to thank for that. Your mission together is complete.

It is time for you to move forward with a new partner for you have many things to accomplish in the coming years.

    Mary Anna

I began digesting the implications of this and rearranging the pieces of my life to accommodate the evolving situation. It is all about our lessons in love. The journey continues...

Wisdom Keepers in the New Paradigm

Harold W. Becker, Founder and President of the Love Foundation is the author of *Unconditional Love - An Unlimited Way of Being*, and *Internal Power: Seven Doorways to Self-Discovery*, along with several other books. He founded The Love Foundation as a nonprofit in 2000. He continues to share his powerful understanding about life through books, consulting, speaking engagements, PBS television specials, workshops and living from his heart.

The Love Foundation is a global nonprofit organization with the mission of inspiring people to love unconditionally. Their vision is to assist people by building a practical foundation and understanding of unconditional love within individuals and society as a whole. Their programs further the awareness and application of unconditional love through education, research, and charity.

Edgar Cayce (March 18, 1877 – January 3, 1945) was an American mystic who allegedly possessed the ability to answer questions on subjects as varied as healing, reincarnation, wars, Atlantis and future events while in a trance. These answers came to be known as "life readings of the entity" and were usually delivered to individuals while Cayce was hypnotized. This ability gave him the nickname "The Sleeping Prophet". Cayce founded a nonprofit organization, the Association for Research and Enlightenment that included a hospital and a university.
He is credited as being the father of holistic medicine and the most documented psychic of the 20th century. Hundreds of books have been written about him and his life readings for individuals. Though Cayce himself was a member of the Disciples of Christ and lived before the emergence of the New Age Movement, some consider him the true founder and a principal source of its most characteristic beliefs.

Filip Coppens (25 January 1971 – 30 December 2012) was a Belgian author, radio host, and commentator whose writings, speeches and television appearances focused on areas of fringe science and alternative history. He was a cohost of the Spirit Revolution radio show, his writing was featured in Nexus and *Atlantis Rising* magazines, and he appeared in 16 episodes of the History Channel's Ancient Aliens television series. He was married to Kathleen McGowan.

David Daida (born March 18, 1958) is an American author who writes about the sexual and spiritual relationship between men and women. His ten books have been published in 25 languages. He conducts spiritual growth and intimacy workshops and is one of the many founding associates at the Integral Institute. He has conducted research and taught classes at the University of California at Santa Cruz, Lexington Institute in Boston, San Jose State University and Ecole Polytechnique in Paris. He is the author of numerous essays, articles, and books on human spirituality including *The Way of the Superior Man*, *Finding God Through Sex*, and *Blue Truth* and the autobiographical novel *Wild Nights*. www.daviddaida.com

Khalil Gibran, 1883 – 1931) was a Lebanese artist, poet, and writer. As a young man he immigrated with his family to the United States, where he studied art and began his literary career, writing in both English and Arabic. In the Arab world, Gibran is regarded as a literary and political rebel. His romantic style was at the heart of a renaissance in modern Arabic literature, especially prose poetry, breaking away from the classical school. In Lebanon, he is still celebrated as a literary hero.

He is chiefly known in the English-speaking world for his 1923 book *The Prophet,* an early example of inspirational fiction including a series of philosophical essays written in poetic English prose. The book sold well despite a cool critical reception, gaining popularity in the 1930s and again especially in the 1960s counterculture. Gibran is the third best-selling poet of all time, behind Shakespeare and Laozi.

Dr. John Mordecai Gottman (born April 26, 1942) is a professor emeritus in psychology known for his work on marital stability and relationship analysis through scientific direct observations, many of which were published in peer-reviewed literature. The lessons derived from this work represent a partial basis for the relationship counseling movement that aims to improve relationship functioning and the avoidance of those behaviors shown by Gottman and other researchers to harm human relationships. Gottman is a professor emeritus of psychology at the University of Washington. With his wife, Julie Schwartz, Gottman heads a non-profit research institute (The Relationship Research Institute) and a for-profit therapist training entity (The Gottman Institute). Gottman was recognized in 2007 as one of the 10 most influential therapists of the past quarter century. "Gottman's research showed that it wasn't only how couples fought that mattered, but how they made up. Marriages became stable over time if couples learned to reconcile successfully after a fight."

David Hawkins, MD, PhD (February 28, 1913 – February 24, 2002) was a professor whose interests included the philosophy of science, mathematics, economics, childhood science education, and ethics. He was an internationally renowned psychiatrist, consciousness researcher, spiritual lecturer, and mystic. Author of more than eight books, including the bestseller *Power vs. Force,* Dr. Hawkins's work has been translated into more than 17 languages. Website: www.veritaspub.com

Gay Hendricks, Ph.D., has been a leader in the fields of relationship transformation and body mind therapies for over 45 years. After earning his Ph.D. in counseling psychology from Stanford, Gay served as professor of Counseling Psychology at the University of Colorado for 21 years. He has written and co-authored (with Katie) 35 books, including the bestseller *Conscious Loving,* used as a primary text in universities around the world. In 2003, Gay co-founded *The Spiritual Cinema Circle,* which distributes inspirational movies and conscious entertainment to subscribers in 70+ countries. Gay has offered seminars worldwide and appeared on more than 500 radio and television shows, including OPRAH, CNN, CNBC, 48 HOURS and others.

Katie Hendricks, Ph.D., BC-DMT, is an artist of life who creates transformational theater events around the world. Passionate about the power of embodied integrity and emergence, she continuously promotes creative expression in service of a direct experience of life, wholeness and evolutionary collaboration. She has been a pioneer in the field of body-mind integration for over forty years. Katie has an international reputation as a seminar leader, training professionals from many fields in the core skills of conscious living through the lens of body intelligence. www.Hendricks.com

Lisa Renee Jones. New York Times and USA Today bestselling author Lisa Renee Jones is the author of the highly acclaimed *Inside Out* series, which is now in development for a television show. In addition to the success of Lisa's *Inside Out* series, Lisa has published many successful titles. The *Tall, Dark and Deadly* series and *The Secret Life of Amy Bensen* series, both spent several months on a combination of the New York Times and USA Today bestselling lists.

Evan Marc Katz. Billed as a "personal trainer for smart, strong, successful women," dating. *By helping women understand men – what they think, how they act, and what they really want –* he empowers them to make healthy, informed choices in love. www.evanmarckatz.com

Sam Keen (born 1931) is a noted American author, professor, and philosopher who is best known for his exploration of questions regarding love, life, religion, and being a man in contemporary society. He also co-produced *Faces of the Enemy*, an award-winning PBS documentary; was the subject of a Bill Moyers television special in the early 1990s; and for 20 years served as a contributing editor at *Psychology Today* magazine. He is also featured in the 2003 documentary *Flight from Death*.

Tom Kenyon, M.A. Tom is a sound healer and has worked as a psychotherapist and counselor for over twenty-five years in private practice, and in 1983 he formed Acoustic Brain Research to scientifically study the effects of sound and music on consciousness and the brain. As a result of his over ten years in brain research, Tom's work is centered around the use of sound and music as a means to create altered states of consciousness for the purpose of accessing the brain/mind's unused potentials.

In addition to his focus on neuropsychology and psychoacoustics, Tom teaches each of the five major systems of transformation: Tibetan Buddhism, Taoism, Hinduism, Egyptian High Alchemy and esoteric Christianity.

Tom teaches workshops and leads tours all over the world. He is the author of the critically acclaimed book, *Brain States*, and the fantasy sci-fi novel, *Mind Thieves*. He also authored *The Hathor Material* and co-authored *The Magdalen Manuscript* with his wife, Judi Sion. He is a featured author in *The Great Shift*. He has produced over 100 CDs and cassettes. www.Tomkenyon.com

Mercedes Kirkel is an award-winning author and spiritual channel for Mary Magdalene and other beings of light. Her recent books, *Mary Magdalene Beckons: Join the River of Love* and *Sublime Union* are available at www.marymagdalenebeckons.com. Mercedes lives in California where she offers workshops and spiritual events, as well as private sessions. Find out more at www.mercedeskirkel.com.

Kathleen McGowan is an acclaimed writer of historical "fiction" of the divine feminine. is the New York Times bestselling author of The Magdalene Line series, novels which explore and celebrate the role of exceptional women in history who have changed the world through their courage. Her novels, *The Expected One*, *The Book of Love* and *The Poet Prince* have been translated into over 40 languages and sold over a million copies. See endnotes for her writings on the Legend of Solomon and the Queen of Sheba.

Michael Mirdad is a spiritual teacher, healer, and author who teaches the awareness of love, light, and Christ consciousness. He has worked as a healer and counselor for over 30 years and is the author of the books *The Seven Initiations of the Spiritual Path*, *Sacred Sexuality: A Manual for Living Bliss*, *You're Not Going Crazy, You're Just Waking Up*, *An Introduction to Tantra and Sacred Sexuality*, *Healing the Heart & Soul: A Five-Step, Soul-Level Healing Process for Transforming Your Life*, and *Creating Fulfilling Relationships*. He has been the Spiritual Leader at Unity of Sedona since 2011. www.grailproductions.com

Ruth Montgomery - Ruth Shick Montgomery (June 11, 1912 – June 10, 2001) was a widely read, well-respected journalist, political columnist and author in Washington, D.C. After her long-time friend and mentor Arthur Ford died of natural causes, Montgomery began automatic writing and was able to communicate with Ford on the other side. Her many books (channeled via automatic writing from her spirit guides) popularized spiritualist notions in public consciousness in the 1960s through the 1990s and paved the way for what is now known as New Age religion.

Michael Newton, Ph.D., holds a doctorate in Counseling Psychology, is a certified Master Hypnotherapist, and is a member of the American Counseling Association. Over many years, Dr. Newton developed his own intensive age regression techniques in order to effectively take hypnosis subjects beyond their past life memories to a more meaningful soul experience between lives. He is considered to be a pioneer in uncovering the mysteries about life after death through the use of spiritual hypnotic regression. He now trains other advanced hypnotherapists in his techniques.

Dr. Newton is the author of three best-selling books, *Journey of Souls: Case Studies of Life Between Lives* (Llewellyn, 1994), *Destiny of Souls: New Case Studies of Life Between Lives* (Llewellyn, May 2000), and *Life Between Lives: Hypnotherapy for Spiritual Regression* (Llewellyn, 2004).

Don Miguel Ruiz, (born 1952), is a Mexican author of Toltec spiritualist and neoshamanistic texts. His teachings are similar to New Age philosophies which focuses on the Ancient Toltec teachings to achieve happiness. Ruiz is listed as one of The Watkins 100 Most Spiritually Influential Living People in 2014. His teaching is significantly influenced by the work of Carlos Castaneda.

His most famous book, *The Four Agreements*, was published in 1997 and has sold around 5.2 million copies in the U.S. and has been translated into 38 languages. The book advocates personal freedom from beliefs and agreements that we have made with ourselves and others that are creating limitation and unhappiness in our lives.

The Four Agreements are:
Be Impeccable With Your Word.
Don't Take Anything Personally.
Don't Make Assumptions.
Always Do Your Best.
He also wrote a companion book to *The Four Agreements*.

Enocha Rangita Ryan Is a transformational healing artist in Sedona for over 30 years, guiding others to their awakenings. She specializes in hands-on healing, massage and bodywork, energy and breath work, the shamanic arts, and spiritual guidance. www.yourheartshome.com

Kenneth Earl "Ken" Wilber II (born January 31, 1949) is an American writer, philosopher, and public speaker. He has written and lectured about philosophy, sociology, ecology, developmental psychology, spirituality and mysticism. His work formulates what he calls Integral Theory. In 1998 he founded the Integral Institute.

Machaelle Small Wright is a nature researcher, teacher, flower essence researcher and developer, and cofounder of Perelandra, a nature research center in the Virginia countryside. Since 1976, she has been working directly with nature intelligences in a co-creative relationship. Machaell's books include: *Behaving as If the God in All Life Mattered*, *MAP: The Co-Creative White Brotherhood Medical Assistance Program*, *Perelandra Garden Workbook: A Complete Guide to Gardening with Nature Intelligences, Perelandra Garden Workbook II: Co-Creative Energy Processes for Gardening, Agriculture and Life, Dancing in the Shadows of the Moon, Co-Creative Science: A Revolution in Science Providing Real Solutions for Today's Health & Environment, Co-Creative Science: A Revolution in Science Providing Real Solutions for Today's Health & Environment,* and *The Mount Shasta Mission.* http://www.perelandra-ltd.com/

Paramahansa Yogananda (5 January 1893 – March 7, 1952), born Mukunda Lal Ghosh (was an Indian guru yogi and guru who introduced millions of westerners to the teachings of meditation and Kriya Yoga through his book, *Autobiography of a Yogi*. Yogananda wrote the *Second Coming of Christ: The Resurrection of the Christ Within You* and *God Talks With Arjuna — The Bhagavad Gita'* to reveal the complete harmony and basic oneness of original Christianity as taught by Jesus Christ and original Yoga as taught by Bhagavan Krishna; and to show that these principles of truth are the common scientific foundation of all true religions.

He said that "The true basis of religion is not belief, but intuitive experience. Intuition is the soul's power of knowing God. To know what religion all is really about, one must know God."

Echoing traditional Hindu teachings, he taught that the entire universe is God's cosmic motion picture, and that individuals are merely actors in the divine play who change roles through reincarnation. He taught that mankind's deep suffering is rooted in identifying too closely with one's current role, rather than with the movie's director, or God. He taught Kriya Yoga and other meditation practices to help people achieve that understanding, which he called Self-realization.

[i] **The Holy Women Around Jesus,** Carol Haenni, Ph.D., page 17 from the Edgar Cayce reading #4 2671. *"Mary Heli, Mary Cleophas and Magdalene stood at the foot of the cross with the Virgin Mary".*

[ii] **The Legend of Solomon and Sheba from the Book of Love**

by Kathleen McGowan, p.40, Simon and Schuster

Makeda, the Queen of Sheba, arrived in Sion with a great retinue, a train of camels, the length of which had never been seen, bearing spices and very much gold and priceless stones, all gifts to the great king Solomon. She came to him without guile for she was a woman of great purity and truth, for she was a woman incapable of pretense or deception. Such things as lies and falsehoods were unknown to her. Thus, it was that Makeda told Solomon all that was in her mind and in her heart and asked if he would answer the questions she had for him. They were not, as some have told, riddles to test his wisdom. Rather they were questions of the heart and soul. His answers would allow her to determine if they were truly born of the same heart and spirit and destined to celebrate the Hieros Gamos together. And yet in the end she did not need these questions. She knew upon coming into his presence and looking into his eyes, that he was part of her from the beginning to the end of eternity.

Solomon was mightily taken by Makeda's beauty and presence and disarmed in total by her honesty. The wisdom he saw in her eyes reflected his own, and he knew immediately that the prophets were correct. Here was the woman who was his equal. How could she be else when she was the other half of his soul?

And so it was that when Makeda, the Queen of Sheba, had seen all the greatness of Solomon, all that he had created in his kingdom and, most of all, the happiness of his subjects, she said to the king, "The report was true that I heard in my own land of your affairs and your wisdom, but I did not believe the reports until I came and my own eyes had seen it, and behold that your wisdom and prosperity surpasses the reports which I heard. Happy are your men. Happy are your subjects who continually stand before you and hear your wisdom. Blessed be the Lord your God who has delighted in you and set you on the throne of Israel! He has made you king that you might execute justice and righteousness. And blessed is the Lord your God who has made you for me and me for you."

And it was then that the Queen of Sheba and King Solomon came together in the Hieros Gamos, the marriage that unites the bride and the bridegroom in a spiritual matrimony found only within divine law. The Goddess of Makeda blended with the God of Solomon in a union most sacred, the blending of the masculine and the feminine into one whole being. It was through Solomon and Sheba that El and Asherah came together again in the flesh.

They stayed in the bridal chamber for the full cycle of the moon in a place of trust and consciousness, allowing nothing to come between them in their union, and it is said in this time that the secrets of the universe were revealed through them. Together, they found the mysteries that God would share with the world, for those with ears to hear.

And yet neither Solomon nor Sheba became a consort of the other, for they were equals, each a sovereign over his and her own domain and destiny. Both knew the time would come when they must separate and return to the duties of their respective kingdoms, and each to stand alone yet again, in newfound wisdom and power. Their triumph and celebration was in what they brought each to the other, to use well and wisely in their individual destinies.

Solomon wrote over a thousand songs following the inspiration of Makeda, but none as worthy as the Song of Songs, which carries within it the secrets of the Hieros Gamos of how God is found through this union. It is said that Solomon had many wives, yet there was only one who was part of his soul. While Makeda was never his wife by the laws of man, she was his only wife by the laws of God and nature, which is to say the law of Love.

When Makeda departed from holy Mount Sion, it was with a heavy heart to leave her one beloved. Such has been the fate of many twinned souls in history, to come together at intervals and discover the deepest secrets of love, but to be ultimately separated by their destinies. Perhaps it is love's greatest trial and mystery – the understanding that there is no separation between true beloveds, regardless of physical circumstances, time or distance, life or death.

Hieros Gamos is consummated between predestined souls, the lovers are never apart in their spirit.

> *For those with ears to hear, let them hear it.*

The legend of Solomon and Sheba Part two as preserved in the Libro Rosso

Hieros Gamos

From Ascension Glossary http://ascensionglossary.com/index.php/Main_Page

Hieros Gamos refers to the "Risen Christos", as the embodiment of the inner Hierosgamic union between the human being and the divine. The Hieros Gamos is the full resurrection of the body to the eternal light of Christos., Cosmic Christ Consciousness. In the bodies return to energetic balance (neutral in the Unity Field or Zero Point), the being is One with God, and the Christos body is glorified in its perfection as representative of God's image. In Hieros Gamos Couplings, the genetic equal of the Monad unites with its counterpart to embody the sacred marriage of Krystic equals, to merge into One spiritual body to hold the Spirits of Christ. A Krystic male and a Krystic Female unite in a Hieros Gamos or Rod and Staff Union as the Christos-Sophia, to be of service within God's Eternal Light divine plan to correct the Sophianic Body and to restore liberation of Ascension upon the earth.

"The term hieros gamos is used generally to refer to the sacred marriage between two divinities, or between a human being and Mother/Father God, or between two human beings (under certain special conditions); the ultimate alchemy of forces which harmonize polar opposites."

This Krystal Star template of which was previously referred to as "Spiritual Marriage in No Time" has returned to the Earth logos in 2012 through the alchemical restoration of the **Hieros Gamos.** Hieros Gamos or "Hierogamy" is the Sacred Marriage of a Human Being with Divinity (the Inner Spirit) and the Unification between all life expressions and its levels of opposite. The planet has reached that axis in time. Hieros Gamos is the sacrament that represents "sacred marriage" at the individual level, to the relationship level, to the group level as a part of spiritual ascension, moving through the spiraling staircase of time to experience unification with (or marry) all aspects of God. When we marry God through this sacrament, Christ returns.

Hieros Gamos is the union of male and female, of matter and consciousness, of flesh and divinity. —Margaret Starbird, "The Woman with the Alabaster Jar,"

About the author

Penelope Genter, "Penny" (1942-)

Mother Mary came to Penny in 1995 and began bringing through messages on her computer that she recorded in book form. That eventually expanded to include others from the higher realms including Merlin, Quan Yin, Archangel Raphael, Archangel Raziel and Archangel Metatron.

Penelope Genter has spent a lifetime studying the face of God and how this is mirrored in all of our relationships. She outlived three husbands and has ten children and stepchildren, sixteen grandchildren, and seven great-grandchildren. She is an accomplished dowser, Master Gardener, and Reiki practitioner. She had her own design business for over 30 years. She produced and marketed flower and gem essences, taught at university and at numerous workshops and seminars.

She is a Unity of Sedona Chaplain and facilitated the Mary Magdalene Circle there for five years. She taught the 16 week *Creating Sacred Relationships Class* at Unity in early 2015 based upon Mother Mary's teachings she channeled. She facilitated a Sophia Woman's group in Sedona from 2015-2017. She taught a class on Reincarnation and Soul Groups at Unity following publication of her book ***Soul Weaving*** in 2018. She now facilitates a Magdalene Mystery School for women in Sedona, AZ.

In 2015 Penny was one of the presenters in the Premier GODTALKS™ presentation in Sedona, AZ. This is available on YouTube and at www.godtalkssedona.com . YouTube also has her talk on **Searching for Mary Magdalene**.

Penelope has written other books with Mother Mary and her partners in spirit that are meant to inspire people to see their own inner divinity and to share this loving awareness with others on the path.

Her most recent books are **Mary Jacobe, Mother of the Way** in which she channels from the akashic records of her life as Mary Jacobe, mother of Mary Magdalene and cousin/mother-in-law of Jesus. And

New Teachings of the Way – Dialogues on Christ Consciousness in the 21st Century with Jesus and Mary Magdalene. Available on Amazon and Kindle, 2019.

Other books by Penelope/Penny Genter

Touching Home—Roadmaps for the New Age with Mother Mary, (E-book) 1998

Returning Home—A Workbook for Ascension with Mother Mary, Merlin and Quan Yin, 2001

2013 Blueprints for the New Paradigm with Archangel Metatron and Raziel and others (E-book) 2007

Sar'h – A story of Tamar, Firstborn of Mary Magdalene and Jesus the Christ, for those with ears to hear available on Amazon, Kindle and Audible. 2017

The Messenger – Healing Breast Cancer – A Path Through Eastern and Western Medicine with Angelic Guidance. Available on Amazon and Kindle. 2018

Women Around the Well – How Sacred Circles of Women are Changing the World. Available on Amazon and Kindle. 2018.

Soul Weaving – Exploring the Tapestry of our Incarnations. Available on Amazon and Kindle 2018.

Woman Warrior – Memories of a Transformative Life. With Eri Shimono. Available on Amazon and Kindle 2018.

Designing the New Paradigm, by Archangels Metatron and Raziel. Available on Amazon and Kindle 2019.

Printed in Great Britain
by Amazon